New Testament Essentials

FATHER, SON, SPIRIT
AND KINGDOM

Robbie Fox Castleman

IVP Connect

An imprint of InterVarsity Press
Downers Grove, Illinois

InterVarsity Press
P.O. Box 1400, Downers Grove, IL 60515-1426
World Wide Web: www.ivpress.com
Email: email@ivpress.com

InterVarsity Press® is the book-publishing division of InterVarsity Christian Fellowship/USA®, a movement of students and faculty active on campus at hundreds of universities, colleges and schools of nursing in the United States of America, and a member movement of the International Fellowship of Evangelical Students. For information about local and regional activities, write Public Relations Dept., InterVarsity Christian Fellowship/USA, 6400 Schroeder Rd., P.O. Box 7895, Madison, WI 53707-7895, or visit the IVCF website at www.intervarsity.org.

All Scripture quotations, unless otherwise indicated, are taken from THE HOLY BIBLE, NEW INTERNATIONAL VERSION®, NIV® Copyright © 1973, 1978, 1984, 2011 by Biblica, Inc.™ Used by permission. All rights reserved worldwide.

While any stories in this book are true, some names and identifying information in this book may have been changed to protect the privacy of individuals.

Cover design: Cindy Kiple
Interior design: Beth Hagenberg
Images: © Pattie Calfy/iStockphoto

ISBN 978-0-8308-1052-9 (print)
ISBN 978-0-8308-9648-6 (digital)

Printed in the United States of America ∞

Library of Congress Cataloging-in-Publication Data

Castleman, Robbie, 1949-
New Testament essentials : father, son, spirit, and kingdom / Robbie Fox
Castleman.
pages cm
Includes bibliographical references.
ISBN 978-0-8308-1052-9 (pbk. : alk. paper)
1. Bible. New Testament—Theology. I. Title.
BS2397.C37 2014
225.071—dc23

2014013398

P	23	22	21	20	19	18	17	16	15	14	13	12	11	10	9	8	7	6	5	4	3	2	1
Y	34	33	32	31	30	29	28	27	26	25	24	23	22	21	20	19	18	17	16	15	14		

Contents

Introduction

The New Testament comprises twenty-seven documents with a long-recognized unique authority for the belief and practice of those who profess a singular allegiance to Jesus of Nazareth as Lord. The New Testament makes clear that Jesus is the incarnate Son of God and the promised Messiah of Israel and Savior of the cosmos. When we study the New Testament, we are bound to wrestle with the greatness of Jesus. The story the New Testament tells confronts its readers with claims that are cosmic in scope and yet are as personally intimate as the relationship between two people who love each other.

The New Testament, like the teaching of Jesus himself, has been and was meant to be translated into the languages of the world from the very beginning. We are meant to still feel the breath of God on our necks in the real world we live in. The documents of the New Testament were first breathed through people living in a particular historical, religious and social context of Palestinian Judaism in the matrix of the Mediterranean cultures of the Roman Empire of the first century. Similar to God's willingness to become fully human in the womb of a young virgin, these God-breathed texts do not begrudge the human fingerprints of its writers.

Four of the books in the New Testament are based on eyewitness accounts (with startling detail!) of the birth, life, teaching, death, resurrection and ascension of Jesus the Christ. Each rendering of the good news (gospel) embodied by Jesus is written to a particular focus audience at a particular time. Three of the Gospel accounts—Mark, Luke and Matthew, in order of writing—follow the same basic outline and are often termed the *Synoptic* (a word meaning "same eye") Gospels.

Two Gospel accounts, those according to Mark and Luke, were written before the fall of Jerusalem in A.D. 70. Most of the documents in the New Testament were written before this watershed date. The Gospel of Mark has a diary-like feel to it in the first half of the book; the account then slows down and the second half of the book recounts the last week of Jesus' earthly life, for the most part. Mark's account has been identified as the memoir of the apostle Peter, and it certainly reflects the feisty personality of the disciple! Like Peter, the Gospel according to Mark jumps right in with the declaration of the good news that Jesus is the Son of God (Mark 1:1). No Christmas story, no backstory at all—by the middle of chapter three, the Pharisees and Herodians are already plotting how to kill Jesus!

The Gospel according to Luke, also written prior to A.D. 70, is full of eyewitness accounts from a variety of people. Luke's account includes details about non-Jews, stories with women as a focus (the account of Jesus' birth through Mary's perspective is only found in Luke), and makes the person of the Holy Spirit in relationship to Jesus more explicit than the other three Gospel accounts. Luke's writing purposefully serves as a witness to non-Jews. On the other hand, the Gospel according to Matthew was written shortly after the fall of Jerusalem. This very Jewish account doesn't begin with the Christmas story but with a long genealogy that begins with "Jesus the Messiah the son of David, the son of Abraham." The Christmas story that follows is focused on the role of Joseph and includes stories important for Jews in the aftermath of Jerusalem's destruction. Matthew is the only Gospel that tells of the visitation of the Magi, the family fleeing to Egypt and Herod's slaughter of Bethlehem's children. It is clear that Matthew's account was intended by God to focus the faith of Israel's people on a Person, not a place.

John did not write his account of the gospel until the last decade of the first century, in the 90s during the reign of the Emperor Domitian. This was during a time of intense persecution by the empire as well as a period when pressure on the early church by unbelieving Jews greatly increased. John's account of the good news begins with the words "In the beginning" as an echo of Genesis 1:1 and so starts with the Word of God before the incarnation of the only begotten Son. John's Christmas story is summed up in a single verse: "The Word became flesh and made his dwelling among us. We have seen his glory, the glory of the one and only Son, who came from the Father, full of grace and truth" (John 1:14). Ninety percent of John's account is unique to the Gospels, and it is clear by what is included and what is left out that he is very aware of the content of the other accounts that had been circulating for decades.

I've often told my students in the classroom that the four Gospel accounts in the New Testament are like four kinds of stew. The same "meat and potatoes" are found in each, but the broth is distinct for God's own purposes in breathing this story of Jesus in quadraphonic fashion for the salvation of the world. Like the Gospels, it is important to read each document in the New Testament with an understanding of its original audience and time.

The book of Acts, the second volume of Luke's masterful work, tells the story of the early church and its spread from Jerusalem to the ends of the earth within thirty years of Jesus' death, resurrection and ascension. The last document of the New Testament, the book of Revelation, focuses on a series of visions John was instructed to record to first help the church during the reign of Domitian to be faithful to Christ Jesus. However, like all the New Testament documents, it is a living word and its first focus does not confine its relevance or application to its first audience alone. Every book in the New Testament was intended to be heard throughout the ages. Like John, all twenty-seven books of the New Testament are written "that you may believe that Jesus is the Messiah, the Son of God, and that by believing you may have life in his name" (John 20:31).

The other twenty-one "books" of the New Testament are actually letters written to particular people in particular situations at a particular time, and probably all but the letters of John were written before the fall of Jerusalem. Taking into account the where, when and why of the letter writer and the intended first recipients can help insure that our contemporary understanding and application of the text stay connected to the God-breathed intention for its original audience. The study of Scripture must be done with significant integrity—stick to the text and work to hear it in its own historical and cultural context first. This discipline helps minimize reading our own culture, history and experiences into the text. The first movement in biblical studies is from *exegesis* (reading out of the text) to the interpretation of what it meant "then and there." Then and only then are we ready for the next movement from "then and there" to "here and now." Any response to God's Word "here and now" must stay rooted in the God-breathed word "then and there."

This study is written to reflect two basic characteristics of the New Testament itself. First, it is Christocentric. Jesus is the point. And, as New Testament scholar F. F. Bruce points out, "the character of Jesus can be known only from the New Testament records."[1] If we don't study and learn about the New Testament Jesus, what Jesus do we follow? Too often people remake Jesus into their own image because it's easier. But the Jesus of the New Testament is far more challenging than most comfort zones allow, and it is with this Jesus we must wrestle. Second, this study is thoroughly trinitarian because this is how God has revealed himself within the arena of creation to his people in the story of Scripture from Genesis to Revelation. God's being, his ontological reality, is that of Father, Son and Holy Spirit in one interpenetrating union of love, will and perfect freedom. The doctrine of the Trinity is grounded in these texts that are the bedrock of God's self-revelation.

This study is organized as a part of the Essentials series and follows a format similar to Greg Ogden's *Discipleship Essentials* and Tremper Longman III's *Old Testament Essentials*. This volume has three parts: the first focuses on the person and work of the Lord Jesus, the second focuses on the person and work of the Spirit in the church's mission in the world, and the third finds its focus on the overarching theme of the kingdom of God as it is present and still to come in the fullness of time as we know it.

Bible Study—Each chapter focuses on particular texts within the New Testament to be read, as well as a verse or two suggested for memorization. This is followed by initial questions to reflect on and discuss with others from your own reading and observation of the text.

Reading—Next, there is a reading section, where I offer background and insights of my own and other scholars concerning the passage or passages and their connection to the canon of Scripture as a whole. The reading is followed by more questions to help you think further about the biblical text.

Connecting to the Old Testament—The reading is followed by a particular connection the New Testament text has to the Hebrew Scripture of the Old Testament.

The Ancient Story and Our Story—The study of the passage ends by considering how the New Testament passage might connect with our own lives today.

I conclude with a short paragraph that helps build a connection to the next study. And at the end of each study I will suggest a supplementary book you might like to read for going deeper.

I was introduced to the gospel of Jesus Christ as a college student. The Jesus of the New Testament overwhelmed me, and by God's grace Jesus still does. It is my hope that Jesus, the Lion of Judah, will roar again and again as you work through *New Testament Essentials*. It is also my hope that Jesus, the Lamb who was slain, will also comfort you as well as confront you every step of the way. Jesus is *the* "essential." Through him we know God as our Father and the Spirit as our Comforter in life and in death. In this hope I dedicate this book to my students. Together we have wrestled with the greatness of Jesus, the wonder of the gospel and the miracle of God's grace.

May each person using this text be awestruck by the New Testament Jesus for the rest of your life. The study of Scripture is an exercise of profound humility. On the day when we see the Lord of glory in his fullness, we will realize that what we studied to understand was but a dim mirror. However, by God's design and grace, it is enough for now.

Ad Majorem Dei Gloriam
Robbie Fox Castleman

---

[1]F. F. Bruce, *The New Testament Documents: Are They Reliable?* (Downers Grove, IL: InterVarsity Press, 1981), p. 3.

Part One

THE REVELATION OF GOD IN JESUS CHRIST

1 / Jesus, the Messiah

LOOKING AHEAD

MEMORY VERSE: Mark 8:34-35
BIBLE STUDY: Mark 8:27–9:8
READING: Learning to Recognize the New Testament Jesus

Messianic expectations in Second Temple Judaism (the time from the postexilic rebuilding that began with Haggai in 520 B.C. to the destruction of Jerusalem in A.D. 70) centered on a new leader to deliver Israel from its occupying enemy, the Roman Empire.[1] They were not expecting a Galilean rabbi who stood on a hilltop and said, "Love your enemies." Consider this as you read through this study's text.

 Bible Study Guide

After reading Mark 8:27–9:8, spend some time reflecting on it with the following questions in mind before looking at the reading.

1. How did Jesus initiate this conversation with his disciples concerning his identity and central mission?

2. Peter focuses on Jesus' identity as the "Christ," the Greek term for the Jewish Messiah, the "anointed one." What do you think Peter's expectations were of the Christ as the anointed Messiah of Israel?

3. Summarize what Jesus indicates as his own messianic expectations (v. 31). _O.T_
- opposite of disciples expectations - a warrior King
- to be rejected / suffer and die at the hands of teachers /
Pharisees...
- no thought of Jesus being Son of God.

How might this description account for Peter's rebuke (v. 32)?

4. Notice that this rebuke in Mark's Gospel is not explained in any detail. Compare Mark 8:32 with Matthew 16:22, which includes a bit more of Peter's objection. How would you summarize Peter's central concern?

5. How does Jesus' reaction to Peter indicate the significant differences between the messianic expectations of Peter and Jesus' own?

Jesus - suffering / serving / loving

How does the teaching of Jesus that follows (Mark 8:34–9:1) address the contrast between Jesus' mission and expectations of Israel for their Messiah?

6. How do Jesus' description of his mission and the expectation of those who follow Jesus as God's anointed one contrast with that of Satan and his expectations and desires?

How is this dynamic still a problem and a temptation for those who consider themselves Jesus' disciples today?

Jewish view of salvation -
Salvation for a people/a nation
Jewish beliefs of afterlife - done
didn't believe in it.

7. In all three Synoptic Gospels the transfiguration of Jesus follows this challenging teaching of Jesus near Caesarea Philippi. How might the transfiguration experience have been particularly helpful and meaningful for Peter after Jesus' stern reaction to the disciple's rebuke and the challenging teaching that followed?

8. What is Peter's initial response to the transfiguration?

To build a shelter/contain it

How does the declaration of God the Father (Mark 9:7) continue answering the question Jesus asked in Mark 8:27?

How might the experience of seeing the transfiguration of Jesus help the disciples adjust their expectations of his mission in the light of his teaching and his identity?

9. In the light of this Scripture study, how might disciples and congregations today still struggle with the person and message of the New Testament Jesus?

× Diff. views/opinions in Jewish faith around salvation/ resurrection...
- Parcels they agreed on - to be from there (King David) to save the world

👓 Reading: Learning to Recognize the New Testament Jesus

The narrative account of Jesus and his disciples as they journey near the area of Caesarea Philippi is the centerpiece of the Synoptic Gospels. The story's placement within the Synoptic Gospels is right in the middle of each account, and this reflects the pivotal importance of how the first followers of Jesus struggled to come to terms with Jesus' identity and mission. The word *synoptic* means "with one eye" and indicates how Matthew, Mark and Luke follow the same narrative sequence of events in the life of Jesus, with approximately the first half of each of these Gospels devoted to Jesus' public ministry in Galilee. The second half of the Synoptic Gospels is devoted to the last week of Jesus' earthly life and ministry in and around Jerusalem in Judea. If you were to sit down and read each of the Synoptic Gospels in one sitting you would notice that nearly all the miracles of Jesus occur before this episode near Caesarea Philippi. This also indicates how the narrative account of Jesus' teaching at Caesarea Philippi is pivotal if one is to understand who Jesus is and what he came to do.

The city of Caesarea Philippi was located about twenty-five miles north of the Sea of Galilee near one of the headwaters for the Jordan River. Herod the Great had been designated the ruler of this region originally by Caesar Augustus in 20 B.C., and upon Herod's death his son Philip was willed the districts of Iturea and Trachoni-tis (see Luke 3:1), which included the Paneas, the site of Caesarea Philippi and its surroundings. The term *Paneas* designates the ancient history of the place, which included a cave in a nearby mountain that had been dedicated to Pan, the Greek god of nature. The population of the area was predominantly non-Jewish. In addition to its lingering paganism, Jewish presence in Paneas was minimized for historical reasons. It was in Caesarea Philippi that the infamous Seleucid general Antiochus IV was victorious over Egypt in the second century B.C. and gained control of all of Palestine with disastrous results. Antiochus IV persecuted the Jews of Palestine, approved of the desecration of the temple in Jerusalem, and intentionally slaughtered Jews on the sabbath when they would not defend themselves in an attempt to keep sabbath law. However, it is in this area known for its long-standing paganism and the persecution of Jews that Jesus is first proclaimed the Messiah!

As surprising as the site of this proclamation is, it is entirely fitting that Jesus initiates a discussion of his identity and mission in a place known for false gods, fanatic bigotry, violence and the oppression of God's people. Jesus' question (Mark 8:27) prompts the typical response. The mention of Elijah, John the Baptist and one of the prophets (v. 28) is an echo of Mark 6:14-16 when others speculated on

Jesus' unusual authority and works of wonder, which were well known among the common population at the time. But Jesus presses the question further when he asks for the disciples' own opinion of his identity (Mark 8:29). Peter's reply on behalf of the Twelve is the first time in Mark's Gospel that someone besides demons or God declares that Jesus is the Messiah, the anointed One of Israel.

Jesus then proceeds to radically redefine what it means to be the Messiah (vv. 30-31) and the disciples and their spokesperson, Peter, find Jesus' redefinition unrecognizable in the light of their own expectations for Israel's Messiah. Palestinian Jews of the first century expected a Messiah to be more like a Maccabee! It was the Maccabees, just a few generations before, who opposed the Seleucids, the ruling military power in Palestine after the death of Alexander the Great, by organizing a guerrilla army that proved triumphant and resulted in 103 years of Jewish independence for Israel. This independence ended in 63 B.C. when the Roman Empire conquered Palestine. First-century Jews were looking for the son of David, the seed of Jesse, the promised Messiah, to be a warrior king who would deliver Jerusalem from the Gentiles and reestablish and protect an everlasting kingdom for God's own people. Jesus' disciples were looking for a Messiah who conquered their enemies, but instead Jesus stands on a hillside and talks about loving one's enemies. And here in Caesarea Philippi Jesus talks about the Messiah as the "Son of Man" (v. 31) who

must suffer, be rejected by the very people most disciples would esteem above all others, and die. No wonder Peter takes "the Messiah" aside and begins to rebuke Jesus for such unmessianic ideas!

It's interesting to note that when Jesus, in return, rebukes Peter and calls him "Satan" (a Hebrew word meaning "adversary") he is actually looking at the disciples, not directly at Peter (v. 33). All the disciples were upset, not just Peter. Can you imagine the troubled look on their faces? The anger? The disappointment? The confusion? Jesus' description of his messianic work was completely unimaginable and untenable. How could such weakness possibly provide the power needed to conquer Israel's enemies? How could such foolishness possibly outwit Roman rulers? And how can the most horrendous and shameful means of torture, Roman crucifixion, ever lead to the glorious triumph of God's everlasting kingdom?

When Jesus calls the crowd to join the bewildered disciples (v. 34) the redefinition of his messiahship becomes the explicit description of discipleship for all those who would continue to follow him. This dying to self was a hard call to hear and heed on that day near Caesarea Philippi. And Jesus' demand for discipleship is still so in every "adulterous and sinful generation" (v. 38). The Jesus of the New Testament still says "Get behind me, Satan!" to every want-to-be-follower of Jesus who wants the Christian life to be one of ease, empowerment or a nice shortcut to "the good life" (of course with God's glory as a part of the mix!). This episode on the way to Caesarea Philippi should be hard for us to read today. Like the ending of Jesus' Sermon on the Mount in Matthew 5–7, it is meant to be hard to hear. And like the disciples then, we need encouragement to hold on to and trust that what Jesus says really is the way of salvation and hope and the eternal triumph of God's Messiah and his kingdom.

In all three Synoptic Gospels the account of Jesus' transfiguration follows the devastating unveiling of Jesus as a very unexpected Messiah. Jesus let the disciples struggle with his teaching and their journey as disciples for nearly a week (Mark 9:2), and then three of his disciples got a glimpse that Jesus just might know what he's talking about and that it just might work! These disciples needed to see Jesus glorified in the transfiguration (vv. 2-3), and to note his supremacy in relationship to Moses and Elijah, the historical embodiment of both the law and the prophets (v. 4). And these key disciples needed to hear God's answer to Jesus' question, "Who do you say that I am?" The divine and definitive proclamation, "This is my Son" (v. 7), brought a new dimension to the Messiah that was as unexpected as Jesus' redefinition. The Son of Man was also the Son of God! The transfiguration appropriately ends with the disciples seeing no one but Jesus and the divine admonition still ringing in their ears, "Listen to him!" (v. 7).

Reading Study Guide

Jesus - rejected

~ suffering

1. Write a paragraph that summarizes your understanding of Jesus' identity and mission. Share this paragraph with a friend and ask what is clear or unclear about your summary.

   Jesus' identity was/is his mission. He is saviar and his mission is to save. He reveals God as man and his word and actions reveal God on earth.

2. Note the placement of the Caesarea Philippi episode in the Gospel of Mark. Count how many miracles of Jesus occur before this journey and how many after the episode. How might this distinction enhance the central point Jesus is making clear to his followers?

3. What is a place you are familiar with today that holds similar cultural dynamics (a place known for false gods, fanatic bigotry, violence and the oppression of God's people) to the area of Caesarea Philippi?

   How and why can such a place tempt someone to change or temper his or her witness to Jesus?

4. How are expectations of Jesus today often as wrongly conceived as the messianic expectations of the Jews in the first century?

Bible-study for yourself ~ practice it

5. What can you do in your home and congregation to keep Jesus' demands of disciple-ship clear and uncompromising, full of both grace and truth? *— Radical & risky*

Face your discomfort

6. Like Peter, how have you experienced disappointment in God during times of suffering or struggle?

When have you wanted Jesus to do or say or be something different in times of challenging difficulty?

7. What does it mean for disciples to "deny themselves and take up their cross and follow," to "lose their life for [Jesus] and for the gospel" in order to save it?

What example from your own experience of discipleship might help someone else understand both the gift and the demand of Jesus?

8. How has God encouraged you after a time of struggle and disappointment?

Like Peter during the transfiguration of Jesus, how are both the suffering and glorification of Jesus helpful in regaining hope after hard times?

Connecting to the Old Testament

Jesus, in both his suffering and exaltation, is known as "the son of David." This relationship is more than a recognition that Jesus is a descendent of David in the lineage of Judah (Romans 1:3; Revelation 3:7; 5:5; 22:16), but is also intended to highlight Jesus' willingness to suffer, like David, with the marginalized (1 Samuel 22:1-2; 24:1-12; 26:5-24). Jesus' life is an echo of David's long-suffering with and forgiveness for those who opposed him (2 Samuel 9; 16:5-14; 19:18-23), as well as David's capacity for extending to others the grace and mercy he had received from God throughout his life. Followers of Jesus recognize the power of self-emptying grace: forgiven people forgive. And this is always accompanied by a willingness to suffer for the sake of Christ Jesus. David was a man after God's own heart (1 Samuel 13:14) and is remembered for this in Acts 13:22. David himself, near the time of his death, looks back on his own calling and, at the same time, anticipates the reign of his "son" when he reflects,

When one rules over people in righteousness,
    when he rules in the fear of God,
he is like the light of morning at sunrise
    on a cloudless morning,
like the brightness after rain
    that brings grass from the earth. (2 Samuel 23:3-4)

💬 The Ancient Story and Our Story

It is still essential when we encounter the Jesus of the New Testament that disciples today fix our eyes on Jesus (Hebrews 12:2) and listen to what he has to say. Even when it's not what we expect to hear. Who is the New Testament Jesus? How would you describe the Jesus of the New Testament to a new friend unfamiliar with the Christian faith? What would you emphasize? What might you be tempted to minimize or downplay?

Paul declares in 2 Corinthians 2:17 that those who share Christ with others "are not peddlers of God's word like so many; but in Christ we speak as persons of sincerity, as persons sent from God and standing in his presence" (NRSV). This admonition has several important ideas when we are asked the question concerning the identity of Jesus, "Who do you say I am?" (Mark 8:29).

First, neither Jesus nor the Christian faith is something to sell. There are no fine-print disclaimers, deceptive advertising or alluring practices when it comes to describing the New Testament Jesus to others. Like Peter, we are easily tempted to redefine the person and work of Jesus in easier-to-swallow terms. It is tempting at times to tone down or even eliminate Jesus' teaching about his suffering and the disciple's need to follow Jesus in losing one's life for the sake of the gospel. Consider how the New Testament Jesus and the road to the cross can be neglected, obscured or even eliminated in a service of Christian worship. How are we still prone to share in Peter's rebuke of Jesus for being a suffering Messiah? From the lyrics of songs to the confession of sin to the prominence of the cross in the place of worship or sermon, consider how you, your congregation and its leaders present the person and work of Jesus. If the Spirit would echo the rebuke of Jesus, "Get behind me, Satan," would we have ears to hear? Consider how it's possible today to actually act "ashamed" of Jesus and his words (Mark 8:38) by our representation of Jesus to others. In a culture that celebrates the primacy of numerical growth as a mark of success, it is very easy to become a peddler, a salesperson, a soul winner.

Second, Paul is very conscious that what God thinks of his witness is more important than the response of the person he bears that witness to. As bearers of the "aroma of Christ" we are "captives" to the work and person of Christ revealed in the gospel. And some will think this aroma smells like "death" and others like "life" (2 Corinthians 2:14-16). Easy or not, we, like Paul, must remember "we speak before God with sincerity" (2 Corinthians 2:17) and therefore our witness must be honest, thoughtful and as full of truth as it is of grace. You might recall the story in the gospel of the rich young ruler that walked away from Jesus because he couldn't risk losing his life or his livelihood (Mark 10:17-30; Matthew 19:16-29; Luke 18:18-30). Although saddened by the man's decision, Jesus let him walk away. Jesus didn't run after him to make a different offer, another deal or an easier and more accommodating alternative to discipleship. Consider how easy it is for us to make the gospel's demand something other than an invitation to follow the New Testament Jesus, to lose one's life and to really live.

Take time this week and for the rest of your life to continue your study of Scripture and rediscover over and over again the Jesus of the New Testament, who issues a costly call to follow him. Salvation by faith alone is through grace alone by the work and person of Christ alone. And it costs us everything. Always has, always will.

LOOKING AHEAD

The challenge of discipleship as a journey of dying to self is central to the New Testament witness of both Jesus' life and the ongoing mission of the Spirit in the life of every believer. The same challenge of Jesus at Caesarea Philippi in the Synoptic Gospels is also found in the Gospel according to John when "the Greeks" or non-Jews expressed an interest in meeting the Jewish Messiah (John 12:20-26). Later Paul will underscore Jesus' challenge to the disciples at Caesarea Philippi when he writes about the weakness and foolishness of the cross being greater than human power and wisdom (1 Corinthians 1:18-30). This pivotal teaching is reflected in many New Testament passages in a variety of situations and cultural contexts we will consider in studies based on Romans 8, Philippians 2 and 1 Peter 1. In study 2, Jesus makes the cost of discipleship very clear to several people he encounters on his road to the cross.

Going Deeper

To further consider the way of the Savior as the road to the cross, read Dietrich Bonhoeffer's *The Cost of Discipleship* with a friend or small group. Only through Calvary is the victory of resurrection made possible, both for Jesus and his followers.

2 / Jesus, the Lord of Heaven and Earth

LOOKING AHEAD

MEMORY VERSES: John 8:31-32
BIBLE STUDY: Matthew 8:18–9:9
READING: Wrestling with the Authority and Lordship of Christ Jesus

The supremacy of Christ, the unique exclusiveness of allegiance to his absolute lordship and his clear claim to be the Son of God are central to the identification of Jesus in the New Testament. These dynamics created a challenge for those who were confronted by Jesus in the first century, especially for those wrestling with the identity of Jesus as Messiah while considering the cost of discipleship. The demands of Jesus' lordship can create significant challenges for Jesus' followers in the twenty-first century too.

 ## Bible Study Guide

After reading Matthew 8:18–9:9, spend some time reflecting on it with the following questions in mind before looking at the Reading.

Jesus and his disciples had come to the lakeside village of Capernaum (Matthew 8:5), which served as the "headquarters" for Jesus' public ministry in Galilee.

1. What are the five narrative sections, often called pericopes (pronounced pe-rik´-ō-pēz), within this reading? Note the sequence of these stories that take place in Galilee (Matthew 8:1-17) that follow the Sermon on the Mount (chaps. 5–7).

2. How does Matthew identify the first man (Matthew 8:19), who declares his willingness to follow Jesus, and how does this "teacher" address Jesus?

3. What possible connection is there between Jesus' increased popularity and Jesus' decision to leave Capernaum (v. 18)?

   When these men indicate a willingness to follow Jesus as disciples, how does Jesus respond to each (vv. 20, 22)?

4. Notice the contrast of the behavior of the disciples and that of Jesus on the boat during the sudden storm as they cross the lake to the region of the Gadarenes. How does the repose of Jesus (v. 24) connect to Jesus' challenge to the first man who had approached Jesus in Capernaum (v. 20)?

5. Note the sequence of the story in vv. 26-27 and Jesus' address to the disciples. How does Matthew distinguish what Jesus says to the disciples from what he says to the storm?

   How does the passage describe the response of the men in the boat to the authority of Jesus over "the winds and the waves"?

6. Compare the two men that meet Jesus in the region of the Gadarenes (vv. 28-34) with the two men who speak to Jesus in the first pericope. How do the demon-possessed men address Jesus?

7. What does the second question the men ask in verse 29 and the suggestion the men make in verse 31 indicate that the demonic spirits recognize and acknowledge about the identity and power of Jesus?

8. This area of Galilee was a part of the Decapolis, an area with a large Gentile (non-Jewish) population, which probably accounts for the presence of pigs. After the death of the pigs and the deliverance of the two demon-possessed men, what is the response of the pig-herders and the "whole town" to this miracle?

How does the response of the disciples after the storm is calmed (v. 27) differ with the response of the townspeople? (Note that Matthew does not indicate how the two men reacted to their deliverance.)

9. Summarize the story of the paralytic's healing (Matthew 9:2-8). Why do you think Jesus began with his declaration of forgiveness prior to physically healing the man?

(Again, Matthew notes the response of "the crowd," but the response of the man who is healed is barely noted in the text.)

How do the following identify Jesus: the crowd in Nazareth (Matthew 9:8), the demons (Matthew 8:29), the disciples (Matthew 8:21, 25) and the first man to approach Jesus before crossing the lake the first time (Matthew 8:19)?

10. The text of this study has five sequential stories: the teacher and the disciple (Matthew 8:23), the storm (Matthew 8:26), the demons (Matthew 8:32), the paralytic (Matthew 9:7) and Matthew (Matthew 9:9). How do these stories relate to the lordship of Christ Jesus and the cost of discipleship?

👓 Reading: Wrestling with the Authority and Lordship of Christ Jesus

After describing the baptism and subsequent temptation of Jesus, the Synoptic Gospels (Matthew, Mark and Luke) relate the public ministry of Jesus in Galilee. Each Gospel includes either a brief summary or extensive rendering of Jesus' primary teaching followed by stories that focus on several miracles Jesus performed and the encounters Jesus had with people. The surge in Jesus' popularity is accompanied by an undercurrent of skepticism and resistance by others, most notably some Jewish leaders (for example, see Matthew 9:10-14; Mark 2:13–3:6) and those most familiar with Jesus and his family from his hometown, Nazareth (Luke 4:14-30).

It is understandable that people readily spread the news about the miracle worker and the rabbi who taught with passion, clarity and authority (Matthew 4:23-25; 7:28–9:38; Mark 1:21–3:12). However, people also struggled to understand and accept the very basis of authority by which Jesus taught and exercised miraculous power. One thing to keep in mind when reading the accounts in the Gospels prior to Jesus' ascension is when people addressed Jesus as "Lord" the term does not indicate any insight concerning how they understood who Jesus was (such as in Matthew 8:25). The Greek word translated "lord" (*kyrios*) was a common term used like a polite "sir" as an indicator of basic respect.

Used as an address in the Gospels, the term *Lord* does not mean what it later means in the church after the resurrection and ascension of Jesus as the "Lord of lords, King of kings," who was understood to be the incarnation of God. This is why the frightened disciples can cry, "Lord, save us!" (Matthew 8:25) and continue to be bewildered that a mere "man" (v. 27) could simply speak and a raging storm is turned into a windless calm (v. 26).

One fascinating dynamic of the New Testament is the way each Gospel writer strategically lets every reader wrestle, just as they did, in coming to an understanding of who Jesus really is. Even in the four accounts of Jesus' crucifixion, there is no explanation that Jesus' death on the cross was atonement for sin. This only becomes clear in the rest of the New Testament writings. In fact, it is not until after Pentecost that the disciples begin to connect the dots between what Jesus did and who Jesus is! It is helpful to remember this in order to understand the befuddlement of so many different people in the stories included in this study.

For example, in the first pericope of this study (Matthew 8:18-22) Jesus encounters two men who were very impressed with Jesus' ability to cast out demonic spirits "with a word" and to heal "all the sick" (Matthew 8:16). These men were a part of the crowd that gathered at

Peter's home as soon as the sun set when the sabbath observance was over. The first man, a "teacher of the law" (v. 19), was a Jewish scribe skilled in teaching the Mosaic law, yet he wanted to become a student of a miracle-working local rabbi and to follow Jesus "wherever" he went! Jesus let him know right away that following him wouldn't always be as exciting as that night but would include nights of homelessness and uncertainty. The second man, probably standing nearby, also wants to become a student of Jesus, but tells Jesus, "first let me go and bury my father." Jesus' reply clearly indicates the time is now or forget it! At first glance Jesus' response seems grossly unsympathetic and harsh. However, to understand both the man's request and Jesus' response, readers today need to know something about the burial customs of first-century Jewish and Palestinian culture.

It was a significant responsibility, especially for the eldest son in both Jewish and Greek families, to oversee the burial of their father. Some scholars suggest the possibility that the man could essentially be saying to Jesus that he wants to go but can't until his father dies and he is free from this familial obligation. However, the man's language in the text suggests that his father has already died and simply must be buried. The challenge comes because in that culture and time, there was nothing simple to be done after the death of a loved one. Within twenty-four hours of death, a person's body was wrapped in a shroud of cloth embedded with pungent spices, to help disguise the smell of rotting flesh, and placed in a tomb. (This custom is clearly described in the post crucifixion burial of Jesus. The reason the women return to the borrowed tomb on a Sunday morning was because the sabbath observance, which began at Friday sundown, had come to an end at Saturday sundown, and by Sunday morning there would be enough light to see by and they could then add the aromatic spices to the burial shroud.) After a full year, when the flesh had fully decayed, the dry bones left in the shroud would be gathered and put in an ossuary or bone box that would be placed in a niche or on a shelf within the family tomb.

Thus, what this man may have wanted was to put off following Jesus until this was done, and it could have been nearly a year's delay. Last, it was a well-observed custom that the family did not go out to any public place for a full week after the initial burial, so the fact that this man was part of a public crowd in Capernaum may indicate that he was past the time of formal mourning. In light of these customs, Jesus' challenge to the conditions the man placed on beginning his discipleship can be better understood.

Jesus' authority was challenging for people who wanted to use cultural customs to create loopholes to sidestep real obedience, but these stories also indicate the authority Jesus had over the threats of nature, the spiritual realities of unseen powers, human suffering and sin, and the everyday life of a tax collector. The struggle people had coming to terms with Jesus' authority stemmed from questions about his identity. Matthew wants his readers to wonder with the disciples, "What kind of man is this?" (Matthew 8:27). The struggle to understand Jesus' identity is notable in other ways people address Jesus or refer to him besides "Lord" (Matthew 8:21, 25). The scribe calls Jesus "teacher" (Matthew 8:19), the disciples after the storm (Matthew 8:27) and the crowd after the healing of the paralytic (Matthew 9:8) wonder about this "man." In contrast, the demons occupying the men who lived among the tombs near Gadara recognize Jesus as the "Son of God" with understandable spiritual insight (Matthew 8:29). But, Jesus' self-reference is important to note. The predominant way that Jesus refers to himself in these narratives, as he does in all the Gospels, is as the "Son of Man" (Matthew 8:20; 9:6). Except for the name Jesus, this term is used more frequently than any other in the Gospels and was Jesus' most commonly used self-reference.

The title Son of Man is found in all four Gospels, but only once in the book of Acts (7:56) and in two other New Testament books when quoting the Old Testament (Hebrews 2:6; Revelation 1:13; 14:14). In the Gospels the title is only found in the sayings of Jesus himself. This self-designation for Jesus is used most often when his authority is being questioned or when alluding to his suffering and rejection or when anticipating his vindication and future recognition as the Savior and Judge. The Son of Man clearly points to the reality of the incarnation of God in Jesus of Nazareth, but the title also is used by Jesus to indicate his identification with the messianic figure in Daniel 7, the "Ancient of Days," who in some sense has a divine origin with sovereign authority accomplishing the work and will of God.[1]

It is very clear that Jesus' first hearers understood his self-reference as the Son of Man to have messianic implications that pointed to his authority to teach and act, and they understood Jesus was making clear that this authority was bestowed by the God of Israel himself. This explains the powerful attraction Jesus had for people who left families, fishing boats and tax tables to follow him. It also explains the rejection of his enemies, who began to plot from the earliest days of his public ministry how to put him to death (Mark 3:6; Luke 6:11; Matthew 12:14; John 5:18).

The rest of the New Testament will make clear that Jesus as the Son of Man and Son of God is the Lord of heaven and earth, the Savior of sinners, the Head of the church, and the exalted Christ of God.

---

[1]For more information on the title Son of Man, see I. Howard Marshall, "Son of Man," in *The Dictionary of Jesus and the Gospels*, ed. Joel Green, Scot McKnight and I. Howard Marshall (Downers Grove, IL: InterVarsity Press, 1992), pp. 775-81.

Reading Study Guide

1. What might you think, feel and act in each of the situations in this study (see the following)? Write a summary of each.

   - in Capernaum hearing Jesus' challenge and the cost of discipleship as an eavesdropper (Matthew 8:18-22)

   - in the boat during the storm raging and then stilled only by Jesus' word (Matthew 8:23-27)

   - in the presence of two violent, demon-possessed men as a pig-herder or townsperson (Matthew 8:28-34)

   - in the home in Nazareth as one of the friends of the paralyzed man who may have known the connection between his sin and his injury (Matthew 9:1-8)

   - in line at Matthew's tax booth when the hometown rabbi suddenly disrupts business (Matthew 9:9)

2. Think about the various titles used for Jesus in the reading for this study. Summarize what you mean when using the title that is most familiar to you. How does your daily life of discipleship reflect this understanding?

3. Read Matthew 8:1-17 and Matthew 9:2-38, the passages just before and after the texts we considered in this study. Compare and contrast these stories to those already studied.

   • Who are the people Jesus meets?

   • How is each person engaged by Jesus and what is their response to Jesus?

   • What does Jesus say in each passage about the situation and about himself?

4. Think about what it may have been like to have been a person who listened to Jesus' teaching in the Sermon on the Mount (Matthew 5–7) and then followed him down the mountain to Capernaum, across the lake and back again; to the banquet at Matthew's house; hearing Jesus' conversation with the disciples of John the Baptist; seeing the synagogue official's daughter raised from the dead; witnessing the healing of a long-infirm woman, two blind men and the exorcism of a man who was mute; and going with Jesus "through all the towns and villages . . . [hearing Jesus proclaim] the good news of the kingdom and healing every disease and sickness" (Matthew 9:35). When at last you heard Jesus say, "The harvest is plentiful but the workers are few. Ask the Lord of the harvest, therefore, to send out workers into his harvest field" (Matthew 9:37), what would you pray?

What would you do?

5. It is not difficult to understand that the disciples "were amazed" when Jesus stilled the storm (Matthew 8:27) or why the crowd was "filled with awe" after the healing of the paralyzed man (Matthew 9:8), but there is only one time that the Gospels record Jesus being "amazed" by someone and his faith. This unique reaction of Jesus concerns the faith of the Roman centurion just before the passages considered in this study (Matthew 8:5-13). Read this story in another Synoptic Gospel, Luke 7:1-10. Why was Jesus amazed at this man's faith?

How does the faith of this man relate to Paul's understanding of what it means to "live by faith, not by sight" (2 Corinthians 5:7)?

How does this relate to your faith in following Jesus today?

 Connecting to the Old Testament

The "Bible" for God's people in the first century was, of course, the Hebrew Scriptures of the Old Testament. The Old Testament had been translated into Greek during the middle part of the third century B.C. and is the only version of the Hebrew Scripture quoted in the New Testament. The Greek Old Testament is known as the Septuagint (pronounced sep´tōō ə jint), which means "seventy," because it was the work of approximately seventy Jewish scholars. This Old Testament translation is often signified as the LXX. In much of

Palestine, Aramaic was the daily language of village life and home, but Greek was the second language of the empire and functioned as the basis of communication, law, commerce, education and politics. For a first-century Jew to know how to read and write Hebrew bestowed "bragging rights" because it was unusual and a sign of religious prestige and academic elitism. When Paul confesses his former life as a Pharisee and his "confidence in the flesh," he mentions that he is a "Hebrew of Hebrews," indicating his fluency in the ancient language of Judaism (Philippians 3:3-6).

The Jews that Jesus encountered knew the stories, songs, commands and prophecies of the Old Testament. These were texts that shaped the sacrificial rites in the temple, messianic expectations, festivals, feasts, worship and, of course, daily discipleship in home and family life. The readings of Torah (the law of Moses) and prophets and the singing or antiphonal recitation of the psalms were part of the regular patterns of practice in the synagogue and the daily prayer times for faithful Jews. The disciples knew God's Word. Much of what Jews anticipated in the coming of God's Messiah was rooted in their reading of the psalms and the prophets. Like people today, their understanding of what they knew varied, but how people responded to Jesus was greatly shaped by their knowledge of God's Word.

Many average Jews knew the psalms by heart for worship, meditation and even for use in daily prayer or during certain religious festivals. Psalm 65:5-8, Psalm 89:5-11 and Psalm 107:21-31 may have been on the hearts and minds of the disciples in the boat during the threatening storm on the lake. These psalms may have influenced the response of the disciples to the amazing power of Jesus, and they may have helped the disciples begin to connect the dots as they began to discern Jesus' identity.

Think about times in your own life when a Scripture story or part of a passage came to mind at a time of crisis or any memorable moment. Making steady progress in understanding God's Word will shape your expectations of God's faithfulness, God's challenges and God's power. God's Word is still the only uniquely authoritative rule of faith and practice that guides the obedience for disciples of Jesus today.

◯ The Ancient Story and Our Story

When reading the Gospels today, it is good to "read them again for the first time." As much as possible, put yourself in the position of being surprised by the story and the person of Jesus Christ. As you meditate on the stories within the Gospels, constantly ask yourself, *If I had been there hearing and seeing this rabbi from Nazareth for the first time, what would I have felt, thought, done? If I didn't know "the rest of the story," what questions would I want to ask? Would I find it easy to believe? How would I react to the challenging demands Jesus makes? How freely would I follow Jesus? What would be my fears, excuses or questions?*

In the first century, messianic expectations were at a fever pitch. Since Israel became a vassal state to the Assyrians (in the eighth century B.C.) and Judah was destroyed by the Babylonians (in the sixth century B.C.), Palestine had been ruled by the powerful empires of Persia and then the Greeks. An indigenous revolt in the mid-second-century B.C. led by a priestly family, the Maccabees, resulted in 103 years of Jewish sovereignty. Then, in 64–63 B.C. the Roman commander Pompey conquered the land in a blitzkrieg from the northern Decapolis to Judea in the south. Josephus, the Jewish historian of the first century, records that the conquest of Jerusalem took one day and cost twelve thousand citizens of Jerusalem their lives. In the aftermath of the Roman conquest, Jews were divided on how best to survive, and eventually prosper once again as a conquered people. Some Jews hoped for a new revolt under the leadership of a military messianic figure like the Maccabees (see Mark 13:21; Luke 17:22-23; John 1:41; 4:25; 7:25-27 for examples of expressions, cautions and confusion concerning messianic hope in the Gospels). Other Jews found it easier to place their hope elsewhere, in accommodation with Rome or working to accrue personal position or wealth. The continuing corruption of the high priesthood and the power of the Sanhedrin council are just two examples of this in the New Testament.

First-century Jewish messianic expectations were as varied as human need and ambition would allow. Empowerment of some kind was the common denominator—be it political freedom, economic advantage, personal wealth or social influence, the Messiah would certainly be a person on a divine mission to vindicate the long-suffering of God's oppressed people. No matter the expectation, Jesus was a surprise to everyone. Who is this rabbi who calls himself the Son of Man with all the messianic authority imaginable and backs the claim with works of miraculous power, and who also stands on a mountain in Galilee and tells those who would join him to love their enemies and do good to those who despitefully use you? No wonder people were conflicted about following or not following Jesus!

This power through weakness, this wisdom through foolishness emerges after the Gospels, after Jesus' resurrection and ascension, after the sending of the Spirit as a major tension that the early church has to address. Jesus as the Son of Man, the Lord of heaven and earth, the Messiah of Israel and hope of the world was first heralded as the Son of God by demons, first seen by the blind, first heard by the deaf, first obeyed by the lame, first understood by children, first worshiped by sinners, first followed by fishermen and tax collectors, first loved by a virgin who gave him birth in a barn. The gospel, the good news of God's love for the world, came in a plain, brown wrapper. And it took a while to see this humble package open and for its glory to be revealed.

LOOKING AHEAD

For Jesus' first disciples the event that *really* connected the dots was the bodily resurrection of the Lord on the first Easter. All that Jesus claimed about himself and all that he had taught and done during his early ministry was vindicated when the women bearing pungent spices for his burial shroud heard these words,

> "He is not here; he has risen! Remember how he told you, while he was still with you in Galilee: 'The Son of Man must be delivered over to the hands of sinners, be crucified and on the third day be raised again.'" Then they remembered his words. (Luke 24:6-8)

This prophecy of Jesus, remembered and shared from the disclosure near Caesarea Philippi (Luke 9:31-32), began to make some sense. Faith was becoming sight. Believing was now seeing as the sun rose on that first day of the week. The Son of Man who had no place to lay his head was the One who made a way to enter the "Sabbath-rest for the people of God" (Hebrews 4:9). The Lord of heaven and earth, who calmed the raging storm, had saved his people from the sea of sin and death. The Exorcist of Gadara had done battle with the evil one and conquered. The paralysis of sin and suffering was ended and the re-creation of the world was begun on that first day of the week. The time had come for God's redeemed people to pick up their mats, leave tax-collecting booths and begin the journey home to the kingdom of God's Son.

In the light of the resurrection, disciples began to answer their question, "What kind of man is this?" But it is good to remember that crucifixion Friday and the silence of Saturday must have been the longest, darkest days Jesus' disciples had ever known. What would it have been like to leave Jerusalem with all your hope and all your expectations of deliverance come to an end in an act of Roman torture? The one you thought might be the Son of Man and the Messiah of God now finds a place to lay his head in a borrowed tomb wrapped in a shroud without spices. What would it be like to walk home thinking, *Were we wrong, completely wrong?*

Going Deeper

Faith that seeks understanding (Anselm's famous *fides quaerens intellectum*) often begins with context and cultural background. One book that is very helpful is *The IVP Bible Background Commentary: New Testament,* 2nd ed., by Craig Keener (InterVarsity Press, 2014). This reference commentary is easy to use because it is arranged in the same order as you find the books, chapters and verses in the New Testament. A second book is *Behind the Scenes of the New Testament* by Paul Barnett (InterVarsity Press, 1990). This book is not a commentary but a very helpful introduction to the background and cultures of the New Testament world.

3 / Jesus' Work

LOOKING AHEAD

MEMORY VERSE: Matthew 5:20
BIBLE STUDY: Matthew 3:13-17; Romans 5:1-11
READING: Christ's Righteousness, Our Present Hope and Future Glory

The fulfillment of righteousness through the obedience of Christ Jesus is manifest in Jesus' baptism, his sinlessness through temptation, his obedience unto death, his vindication by God through the resurrection and his glorification by God in the ascension.

Bible Study Guide

After reading Matthew 3:13-17 and Romans 5:1-11, spend some time reflecting on it with the following questions in mind before looking at the Reading.

1. Note how John the Baptist deflects his sense of status compared to that of Jesus (Matthew 3:13). What is Jesus' main point in his reply to John the Baptist (v. 15)?

2. Jesus does not disagree with John's argument regarding status in submitting himself to John's baptism. What is the connection between the baptism of Jesus and the whole story in Scripture of human need for God's gift of righteousness in salvation (Matthew 3:15)?

3. What was the aftermath of Jesus' baptism after he "went up out of the water" (v. 16)? Note the dynamic of the Trinity in this passage and how God is fully present as Son, Spirit and Father.

4. How does the memory verse for this study (Matthew 5:20, a central point in Jesus' Sermon on the Mount) echo Jesus' understanding of both human need and Jesus' fulfillment of righteousness (Matthew 3:15)?

5. What are the connections between the baptism of Jesus to fulfill all righteousness and the ultimate reconciliation that Jesus' death makes possible (Romans 5:1-11)?

What is the connection between "hope" and "glory" in Romans 5:2, 5?

6. Note the repetition of "through our Lord Jesus Christ" in Romans 5:1, 11. What are the things in this passage that are obtained "through our Lord Jesus Christ"?

7. List the sequence of sanctification in Romans 5:3-4. How do the sequences in 1 Peter 1:6-7 and James 1:2-4 concerning faith, suffering, perseverance and glory compare to the sequence in Romans 5?

8. Note the dynamic of God the Father, God the Son and God the Holy Spirit in Romans 5:1-11. How is the love of God, explicitly mentioned in verses 5 and 8, connected to the Spirit and the Son?

9. Summarize the condition of humankind Paul notes three times in Romans 5:6, 8, 10. What does God do for us in the face of each reality?

10. Note the past, present and future dynamics in Romans 5:9-11. Consider how the person and work of Christ Jesus in the *past* (incarnation, suffering, death, resurrection and ascension) relate to the *present* reality of salvation through the righteousness of Jesus' baptism and being made right, "justified by his blood" (Romans 5:9). How then do these dynamics relate to the hope of *future* glory and the fullness of salvation to come?

Reading: Christ's Righteousness, Our Present Hope and Future Glory

Speaking of Jesus, Paul writes, "God made him who had no sin to be sin for us, so that in him we might become the righteousness of God" (2 Corinthians 5:21). In this startling statement Paul summarizes the connection between the baptism of Jesus "to fulfill all righteousness" (Matthew 3:15) and the death of Jesus for the "powerless" (Romans 5:6), "sinners" (Romans 5:8) and "enemies" of God (Romans 5:10), which secured the only "access by faith into this grace," our present reconciliation and hope and our future salvation and glory. Only "through our Lord Jesus Christ" (Romans 5:1, 11) and the perfection of his obedience to God in his incarnation, baptism and crucifixion does his righteousness become ours by faith through the gift of God's great grace.

How have you responded to (or might respond to) the following question: When were you saved? Many would naturally tell of a time when a parent prayed with them as a child or a particularly memorable moment with a youth group leader, pastor or a friend at a special event, conference or retreat. More than a few would recall a special service of worship, an altar call or time of quiet, a moment alone that profoundly reordered their life. Surely, all of these and many other stories of time and place are important beginning milestones in one's faith journey. They are significant moments to God too. But these moments

do not answer the question, When were you saved? As the passages in today's study and throughout the New Testament make clear, salvation is grounded in the person and work of the Lord Jesus Christ.

Paul understood when he was a powerless sinner and an enemy of both God and his people in the early church that Christ died for him. Paul answers the question of salvation clearly when he writes,

> I have been crucified with Christ and I no longer live, but Christ lives in me. The life I now live in the body, I live by faith in the Son of God, who loved me and gave himself for me. I do not set aside the grace of God, for if righteousness could be gained through the law [one's own effort to attain right standing with God], Christ died for nothing! (Galatians 2:20-21).

When was Paul saved? When was our salvation secured? On the cross of Jesus.

The cross of Jesus was the ultimate work of God "to fulfill all righteousness." This ultimate work began in the incarnation of the Son and his identification with human sin through his baptism. This work of the incarnate Son was tested through temptation, frailty, fatigue, suffering and torture. The fulfillment of righteousness and the salvation of God was the work of Christ Jesus and in him alone is faith rightly placed. "Therefore, since we have been justified through faith, we have peace with God through our Lord Jesus Christ, through whom we have gained access by faith into this grace in which we now stand" (Romans 5:1-2).

The phrase *justified through faith* must be carefully considered. Paul's focus here isn't faith in his own experience on the road to Damascus or his baptism by Ananias (Acts 9), but on what Jesus himself had done, especially on the cross, to make a way for him (and by extension all those who put their *faith in the work and person of Christ*) to "gain access" to the lavish grace of God's love. In the same way the timing or means of our own baptism or our story of surrender to the Savior, as significant as these are to each of us, is not the ultimate focus of salvation. Our story of God's grace is but a precious part of God's great work of salvation "through our Lord Jesus Christ" in whom we now have "peace with God" (Romans 5:1) and "through whom we have now received reconciliation" (Romans 5:11).

"Peace with God" now is the source of one's hope for future glory that stands the test of suffering, not by our own effort but by the love of God "poured out into our hearts through the Holy Spirit" (Romans 5:2-5). The Greek word for peace Paul uses isn't just the absence of conflict—the cross isn't just about "being saved from God's wrath" (Romans 5:9), which is good news in and of itself! However, to view the work of Christ this way is to limit God's love to an act of mere *mercy*, not getting what one fully deserves. In addition to

God's mercy, "peace with God" includes the wonder of divine *grace*, getting what one absolutely does not deserve—the love of God poured out, overflowing, lavishly slathered upon us. Paul's idea here echoes the Hebrew idea of God's *shalom*, God's welcoming rest, the fullness of his presence and blessing that makes a way for human flourishing, deep joy and access to the very "grace in which we now stand" (Romans 5:2).

In this peace, the lavish outpouring of the *shalom* of God, we experience even in the midst of suffering or hardship the joy of reconciliation with God himself. The fulfillment of righteousness through Christ Jesus has become our righteousness; we are made right with God now and forever. For the sake of sinners, the enemies of God, powerless to gain their own righteousness, Jesus submitted to baptism by John in the Jordan, and the long walk to Calvary's cross began so that all righteousness might be fulfilled. Hallelujah, what a Savior!

The wayward and rebellious son in the parable found in Luke 15 was willing to settle for his father's mercy—just to get out of the pigsty and work as a hired hand would be good enough (see Luke 15:11-32 to read the "Parable of the Lost Son"). But mercy was not enough for the young man's father! No, the father runs to meet his son when he sees him down the road, hugs him tightly, kisses him, puts the best robe around his shoulders, a ring on his finger and even throws him a welcome-home party! The son would have gladly settled for the mercy of a safe place and enough to eat—"just a room over the garage, Dad, and a little work to get back on my feet—I'm just glad you aren't angry." But the father ushers his son into the house to his own room and a welcome that said, "Oh, son, I thought you were dead and lost and now here you are, alive and where you belong! Angry? Not a bit, what is past is past—welcome home to be loved as my son!"

The fulfillment of God's righteousness always goes beyond mercy to the fullness of divine love. The memory verse for today, Matthew 5:20, hints at the utter impossibility of this righteousness apart from the work of God through Jesus Christ. In the Sermon on the Mount Jesus concludes his point that all that the prophets have foretold and the law demands will be fulfilled in him (Matthew 5:17) when he states, "I tell you that unless your righteousness surpasses that of the Pharisees and the teachers of the law, you will certainly not enter the kingdom of heaven." If you had been sitting on the hillside that day, either as a religious professional or just the average faithful Jewish believer, this challenge would have shaken your hope of salvation to the core of your being—especially as Jesus equates anger to murder and lust to adultery! The word Jesus used for "surpasses" is a word that means "that which exceeds the very best of one's own efforts"—something that is beyond one's reach even if on tiptoe with arms and fingers stretched to the maximum limit. Only in the fulfillment of all righteousness in Christ Jesus, when his righteousness is given as a gift of God's grace, are we made fit to belong at home in the kingdom of God.

Reading Study Guide

1. Just before his ascension Jesus commissions the disciples to "go and make disciples of all nations, baptizing them in the name of the Father and of the Son and of the Holy Spirit, and teaching them to obey everything I have commanded you" (Matthew 28:19-20). How are Jesus' baptism, teaching and disciple-making in Matthew 3:13-17 and Romans 5:1-11 reflected in this commission of Jesus at the end of Matthew's Gospel?

2. The "when" and "how" of baptism often overshadow the focus on Jesus as the "who." Make time to talk to an elder in the faith that is a part of your church or denominational tradition, like a pastor, teacher or other congregational leader, about how to understand your own baptism as a participation by faith in the baptism of Jesus.

3. In both passages in today's study the Trinity of Father, Son and Spirit are evident. How do you experience the persons of the triune God in prayer, worship, mission and witness in your own life?

4. *Mercy* is not getting everything we deserve, and *grace* is receiving what we absolutely do not deserve. Mercy is like a father one afternoon letting a child out of a thirty-minute time-out in twenty minutes; grace is the same father taking this child out for ice cream after dinner. What is another way to illustrate and explain both the distinction and connection between mercy and grace?

5. Reread Romans 5:1-11 and write a letter to God expressing your understanding and gratitude for this summary of the gospel of Jesus Christ.

6. Write your own "translation" of Romans 5:1-11 using your own words that reflect your understanding of peace, faith, grace, glory, suffering, perseverance, hope, righteousness, wrath, sin, reconciliation and salvation—write as if you want to explain what you believe to a child in grade school.

7. Read the Sermon on the Mount (Matthew 5–7) and make a list of questions you would have wanted to ask Jesus if you had heard the sermon yourself on that day. In fact, this text in Matthew can be considered Jesus' stump speech for the kingdom that he probably taught many times in many places during his earthly ministry, so it is an essential text to engage over and over again in the journey of a disciple.

⏩ Connecting to the Old Testament

Paul's understanding of the surpassing righteousness of Christ in relation to the gift of salvation is well summarized when he writes, "God made him who had no sin to be sin for us, so that in him we might become the righteousness of God" (2 Corinthians 5:21). In a letter to Diognetus early in the second century, a church father called this the "sweet exchange."* Sweet indeed!

This sweet exchange of our sin and God's righteousness is a gift of divine grace based solely on faith. This foundational idea is clear in the New Testament and the major point in Paul's very first letter, the letter to the Galatians. In Galatians Paul defends salvation

---

The Letter to Diognetes, chap. 9, in Ante-Nicene Fathers vol. 1, ed. Alexander Roberts, James Donaldson and A. Cleveland Coxe, eds. (Buffalo, NY: Christian Literature Publishing, 1885). The original letter is dated around A.D. 130.

by faith alone through grace alone through Christ alone on the basis of Scripture alone. For Paul "Scripture" was the Hebrew Scripture, the Old Testament, and most particularly the story of Abraham's faith that was accounted to him as righteousness.

Some teachers and leaders in the early church communities in Galatia wanted to add something to faith in Christ Jesus in order to achieve salvation, especially for those who were not Jewish by genealogy or religious practice. These false teachers, called "Judaizers," were a real threat to the gospel because they functioned as Jewish Christians within the early church and therefore had significant influence within congregational communities. These Judaizers maintained that non-Jews (Gentiles) simply had to become Jewish in order to become Christians. To them, this made both historical and religious sense—how can one have a relationship with the one true God of Israel as an outsider? So, faith in Messiah Jesus had to be accompanied by circumcision, sabbath keeping and adherence to Jewish dietary law, at the very least.

However, Paul is outraged at this wrongful appropriation of Abraham's story in the Scripture, because the story makes it very clear that Abraham was declared righteous by God on the basis of faith alone. Paul makes the point in Galatians that both circumcision and the giving of the law came after God's declaration of righteousness on the basis of faith alone. Reading the entire book of Galatians makes this crystal clear, particularly in passages like Galatians 2:15-16; 3:1-9, 17-22; and 5:1-6. In all of this, however, Paul is pointing the Galatians and these false teachers to the story they know very well, the story of Abraham as the father of the Jewish nation and faith.

Abraham's story begins in Genesis 11:27, when he was known as Abram. He marries, but has no children by his wife Sarai, who will be known later as Sarah. The Lord calls Abram to leave his homeland and his people and travel "to the land I will show you" (Genesis 12:1). The Scripture relates simply, "So Abram went, as the Lord had told him" (Genesis 12:4). The story of his nomadic journey takes some time and it is full of trials, problems and the faithful watchfulness of God.

Abraham has an unexpected meeting with "Melchizedek king of Salem" and "priest of God Most High," and the patriarch ends up giving this king of Peace (Salem) a tithe of his spoils of war (Genesis 14:17-20, a story that is central in Psalm 110 and the New Testament book of Hebrews). Shortly after this meeting Abraham prays to God about the continued childlessness of his marriage and his lack of an heir. God reassures Abraham that his wife, Sarah, will bear a son, and through this son Abraham will beget a nation that will outnumber the stars he could see in the night sky (Genesis 15:1-5). Through this son of promise, God will fulfill his first promise to Abraham at the beginning of the story that "all peoples on earth / will be blessed through you" (Genesis 12:3).

So, how did this childless man respond to such an overwhelming and seemingly impossible word from God? The Scripture records simply, "Abram believed the Lord, and he credited it to him as righteousness" (Genesis 15:6). This text is at the center of the New Testament faith that declares God's salvation is a gift of grace by faith alone through "Jesus the Messiah the son of David, the son of Abraham" (Matthew 1:1). This text is the foundation of Paul's argument in Galatians and which he uses again extensively in his letter to the Romans.

The Genesis account concludes with a vivid illustration of how the work of salvation is God's work alone. Genesis 15:7-21 recounts the sacrifice the Lord has Abraham prepare to seal his promise to Abraham concerning his family and their land. The sacrifice is prepared as directed and while Abraham was in a deep sleep (v. 12), the Lord alone in a fiery theophany sealed the covenant of grace through faith: "when the sun had set and darkness had fallen, a smoking firepot with a blazing torch appeared and passed between the pieces [of the sacrificial animals]" (v. 17).

Two thousand years after Abraham there is an echo of this faith of Abraham in the reply of a young Jewish virgin to whom God makes an equally outrageous promise that only he can keep. "I am the Lord's servant," Mary answered. "May your word to me be fulfilled" (Luke 1:38). Later this very story of Abraham is the ending refrain of Mary's song of praise (Luke 1:46-55).

◯ The Ancient Story and Our Story

When Jesus stood on the mountain in Galilee and talked about the righteousness that surpasses even one's best effort and then immediately launched into the startling challenge for faith and life concerning murder and adultery, I've often wondered if Jesus and his audience immediately thought about a story in the Old Testament concerning murder and adultery and the mercy and grace of God. You can read the story in 2 Samuel 11:1–12:23. This story is familiar to many students of Scripture and concerns David's lust, longing and adultery with Bathsheba, which results in the breaking of nearly every one of the Ten Commandments. In the course of things, David tries in a variety of ways (everything from a furlough home from Uriah's duties as a soldier to encouraging drunkenness as a means of marital seduction!) to let Bathsheba's husband, Uriah, think that the pregnancy that resulted from this affair was, in fact, his own child. Nothing worked to cover the pregnancy, and David successfully plotted to have Uriah killed on the battlefield. After a period of mourning, David married "Uriah's wife" (it is interesting to note that this is how the New Testament identifies Bathsheba in Matthew's genealogy—see Matthew 1:6) and she bears David a son. Everything is assumed to be covered up and under control.

However, this point of the story concludes ominously with, "But the thing David had done displeased the LORD" (2 Samuel 11:27). The story nears its conclusion with Nathan the prophet creatively confronting the rather self-righteous David (see 2 Samuel 12:1-7) with his manifold sins and the judgment of his household. David is thoroughly repentant (and writes Psalm 51 as a reflection on this sorrowful tale) and grieves deeply over the eventual death of this young child. The story concludes with this startling note, "Then David comforted his wife Bathsheba, and he went to her and made love to her. She gave birth to a son, and they named him Solomon" (2 Samuel 12:24).

The name Solomon literally means "Peace"—David and Bathsheba have born a "peace child," a child that indicates God is no longer angry, a child of mercy. Bathsheba is not barren, David is not impotent—they have not gotten everything they deserved! In the naming of this second baby, it's as though they know for sure what Nathan had proclaimed, "The LORD has taken away your sin. You are not going to die" (2 Samuel 12:13). God is merciful, and they have peace again. This was enough for David and his wife—the white flag of God's peace, the cessation of hostilities was enough for them.

But it was not enough for God, whose grace goes beyond mercy. Right after the naming of Solomon the text continues with one of the most stunning examples of God's grace in the Old Testament. Speaking of the child, the Scripture says, "The LORD loved him; and because the LORD loved him, he sent word through Nathan the prophet to name him Jedidiah" (2 Samuel 12:24-25). Jedidiah means "beloved by the Lord." Now this is grace. This is the welcome home with a hug, a kiss, a robe, a ring and a party.

Mercy and grace together, in David's story and in ours, yield a surpassing righteousness that not only saves us from the wrath of God but reconciles us as beloved children. This costly, joyful welcome home is the anticipation of Jesus as he entered the waters of the Jordan and the torture of Calvary. This gift grace that surpasses even mercy is what Paul, a violent enemy of God and his people, began to experience on the road to Damascus and as he entered the fullness of Christ's righteousness in his own baptism. This story is the story of every person who has been reconciled by God through faith in the Lord Jesus Christ. God meets us on our own road home and with mercy and grace calls us Jedidiah, for his love has been poured out into our hearts.

LOOKING AHEAD

Study 4 will again look at faith and its relationship to discipleship and obedience in the teaching of Jesus. Like the Sermon on the Mount, the Upper Room Discourse of Jesus is a teaching where the righteousness of Christ bears the fruit of holiness in a believer's life.

Going Deeper

A very short but exceptionally profound book that looks at the essential nature of Jesus as the mediator of everything in a Christian's life is James Torrance's *Worship, Community and the Triune God of Grace* (1997). This InterVarsity Press publication is both pastorally helpful as well as theologically clear as a work robustly built on the gospel and the Scriptures of the Old and New Testaments.

4 / Jesus' Teaching

LOOKING AHEAD

MEMORY VERSE: Matthew 7:24
BIBLE STUDY: John 15:1-17
READING: Believing, Obeying, Bearing Fruit That Lasts

The interrelated nature of faith and obedience is evident in the teaching of Jesus and throughout the New Testament. The fruitfulness of a Christian's life is entirely dependent on God's grace in which the believer remains ("stays put" or "abides") in a relationship of faith in Jesus' own obedience and faithfulness to God. Only in union with Christ Jesus can disciples bear lasting fruit, which is how the Son brings glory to the Father.

 Bible Study Guide

After reading John 15:1-17, spend some time reflecting on it with the following questions in mind before looking at the Reading.

1. John 15:1-17 is a passage that demands several thoughtful readings in order to catch the variety of connections and interrelated ideas in this teaching of Jesus. Read this passage slowly at least five more times, and either in your Bible (or on a printed copy of the passage) use a variety of colored pens (or pencils or markers) to highlight the following words, phrases or expressions:

   - the words *fruit, vine* and *branches*
   - the word *remain* (or *abide*)
   - phrases with the words *command, commands* and *commandments*
   - the phrases *love each other* and other references to love
   - all the references to prayer, asking anything, asking in Jesus' name

   What are your initial thoughts about the passage after completing this exercise?

2. There are seven "I am" statements in John's Gospel. Look up John 6:35; 8:12; 9:5; 10:7, 11, 14; 11:25; 14:6 for the first six statements. List how Jesus identifies himself in each. How does Jesus identify himself in John 15:1, 5?

3. In the Fourth Gospel it is interesting to note that John also includes seven miracles, which the evangelist calls "signs" because they point to who Jesus is in some way. Look up the following passages in John's Gospel and make a list of the seven "signs": John 2:1-11; 4:43-54; 5:1-15; 6:1-14, 16-21; 9:1-12; 11:1-44. How many connections can you make between the "I am" statements and the seven signs?

4. Summarize the distinctions between branches that bear fruit and those that do not in John 15:1-6. How do some fruitful branches come to be more fruitful?

How are branches that yield nothing dealt with by the gardener or vinedresser?

5. What seems to be the relationship of prayer to the bearing of fruit and more fruit (see vv. 7, 16, in particular)?

6. What is the relationship between love and obedience to the commands of Jesus in the passage (note vv. 9-14, 17)?

7. Note how Jesus redefines his relationship with his disciples in verses 14-16. What differences does Jesus want his disciples to understand about this new relationship?

What are the indications of this new relationship to Jesus?

Compare verse 15 with John 13:13. How does this comparison help us understand Jesus' initiation of a new relationship with his followers?

Reading: Believing, Obeying, Bearing Fruit That Lasts

Jesus' teaching known as the Upper Room Discourse is unique to John's Gospel. On the night Jesus was betrayed, he did some highly significant things to help equip his closest disciples for the violence and confusion, disappointment and fear resulting from his impending arrest, trial, crucifixion and death. Jesus also did some things that would only make sense to them after the resurrection or the subsequent sending of the Holy Spirit upon the believers at Pentecost. First, Jesus observed the Passover with his disciples, but in doing so he reshaped the meal that looked back on Israel's deliverance from bondage in Egypt during the time of Moses into a meal that would become a commemoration of his own death celebrating the deliverance of God's people from the bondage of sin. In addition, this meal was initiated not just for reenactment and remembrance but also to embody anticipation for the kingdom that was coming in its fullness (see Mark 14:12-26; Luke 22:7-23; Matthew 26:17-30).

Second, Jesus gave the disciples a model of behavior that they were to have toward one another and a posture of humility and self-giving they were to have in the world. Jesus did this after the Lord's Supper when, like the lowliest of house servants or slaves, he washed the feet of his disciples, including the feet of his betrayer, Judas (John 13:1-17). Third, after Judas Iscariot left to betray the Master and plan his arrest, Jesus, like a lov-

ing parent before a long journey, sat down and had a long talk with his disciples. The Upper Room Discourse is full of warnings and advice, as well as a few commands, prophecies and promises. Jesus understood that his disciples would not understand much of what he had to say, but he knew as events unfolded, and especially after the sending of the Spirit, that they would begin to understand what he meant. Jesus explicitly states this recognition of his own need to teach and tell the disciples very hard-to-hear things, as well as the limits of the disciples' understanding, when he says, "I have told you this, so that when their time comes you will remember that I warned you about them. I did not tell you this from the beginning because I was with you, but now I am going to him who sent me" (John 16:4-5).

Last, Jesus concludes this time of teaching (see John 13:31–16:33) with prayer (often designated Jesus' "High Priestly Prayer") in the Upper Room (John 17) and another season of personal prayer in the Garden of Gethsemane just before his arrest (see Mark 14:32-42; Luke 22:40-46; Matthew 26:36-46). In all of these things we can sense a tender and truthful, affectionate and yet time-to-grow-up fond farewell between Jesus and his closest disciples. It is clear that Jesus' last "I am" statement as the "true vine" and his identification of the disciples as fruit-bearing branches is meant to help the disciples cling to Jesus in the coming days, which will befuddle and frighten them. Jesus, of course, knows that by his passion these beloved disciples are about to be painfully pruned to be even more fruitful, and they need to be encouraged to trust him and hold tight even in the darkest hour.

As noted in the study section, Jesus' command to "love one another" is an important focus of John 15:1-17, and Jesus actually begins the Upper Room Discourse with this admonition: "A new command I give you: Love one another. As I have loved you, so you must love one another. By this everyone will know that you are my disciples, if you love one another" (John 13:34-35). What parent has not said to their older children when left alone for the first time, "Now, behave while I am gone, don't fight, and I'll be right back"? That's the basic dynamic of the Upper Room Discourse in a small nutshell!

In the passage for this study, note how many times the word *remain* (or *abide*) occurs. In the original language the word that is used supports the idea of someone who is in a close and settled union with another—the idea of deep connection without resistance or impatience. I've often thought that to "remain" or to "abide" in this sense means to rest confidently, without a hint of fidgeting, in the embrace of someone who loves you.

It is within this intimate confidence and below-the-surface knowing and understanding of someone that one is free to "ask whatever you wish" (v. 7), because it will line up accordingly with the will of the one who holds you in such a contented embrace. This is what Jesus means by

"whatever you ask in my name the Father will give you" (v. 16). To ask the Father for anything the Son would ask is the best way to receive the gift of answered prayer. It is vitally important to note that Jesus ends this thought with the command "Love each other" (v. 17). One of the best ways Christians can love each other is through intercessory prayer, asking God to give good guidance, wisdom, endurance—all good things—according to his will for brothers and sisters who share the life of Christ Jesus by the Spirit.

Indeed Jesus' command to love may cost us more than prayer. He says, "My command is this: Love each other *as I have loved you.* Greater love has no one than this: to lay down one's life for one's friends" (vv. 12-13). The verb "lay down" in the original language is part of a word play hard to discern in a language other than Greek, but it literally means "to set aside." Those who follow Jesus are to "set aside" their lives for the sake of others, not just in the possibility of death but in daily life. Like the example Jesus set in taking on the job of the lowliest Jewish or Roman house servant or slave when he washed the feet of his disciples, Jesus "took off" (or "laid aside") his outer clothing (John 13:4) in order to "wrap a towel around his waist" to wash the disciples' feet. The word used in chapter 15 for "lay down" is from the same root word John uses to describe Jesus' act of laying aside his garment to take on the role of a servant for his friends, even the friend who he knew would betray him. "No greater love" indeed.

Reading Study Guide

1. Consider the relationship that Jesus highlights between remaining in his love and his word (John 15:7, 9-10). What might be your next best step in being a student of Scripture in order to grow in how you love your family, friends, faith community and world?

2. Reflect on areas in your life where you find it hardest to obey the command to love without thought of self, to "lay aside" your own interests. Consider your congregational community and its strengths and areas of weakness when challenged to love like Jesus loved. What makes this most difficult and why might this be?

3. Keep a journal or a time log for a month to help assess your practice of and commitment to praying for others. What might be a good next step to enrich your practice of praying well?

4. Think about your sense of calling to be a follower of Jesus (John 15:15-16). How does the reality of being chosen by God for the lifelong journey of discipleship change the way you respond to the demands and joys of routine daily life?

5. Take a week and read the Upper Room Discourse teaching section (John 13:31–16:33) every day without taking notes or having a sense of "study"—just listen quietly, soak it in. During the next week, read small sections of the discourse prayerfully. How might you best abide in this word?

How can you obey and love in the light of what you are learning?

6. Take a week and read through Jesus' High Priestly Prayer in John 17 every day. After time, note the following:

- How does Jesus address the Father in the prayer?

- What does Jesus ask for himself in the prayer?

- How does Jesus pray specifically for his disciples (including you!—see v. 20) in the prayer?

- How might this prayer of Jesus help shape and inform your own prayers for yourself and for others?

Connecting to the Old Testament

Israel had failed in great measure as a fruitful vine, as the prophets noted (see Isaiah 5:1-7; 27:2-11; Jeremiah 2:21; 12:10-13; Ezekiel 15:1-5; 17:1-21; 19:10-14; Hosea 10:1-2). The psalmist and prophet Asaph anticipates the day when the Son of Man, the Messiah, would prove to be the "true vine" (Psalm 80:8-18).

Jeremiah was a prophet of God during a turbulent time in Judah's history. The prophet's warnings (as well as those of Isaiah and other prophets) concerning the neglect of justice and the tolerance of idolatry fell on deaf ears and hard hearts. Jeremiah was severely persecuted by Judah's kings and false prophets during the time he persisted in telling the truth of God's impending judgment. At one point Jeremiah was thrown into the muddy bottom of a cistern to die, out of sight, from starvation (see Jeremiah 38).

However, the true prophets, like Jeremiah, proved to speak the truth and the judgment of God came through the conquest of the land by the Babylonians. The Babylonian Empire attempted, with some success, the cultural conquest of God's people by forcefully exiling Judah's leaders and many citizens. Only a small percentage of God's people would ever return to the land of Palestine when this was permitted after the Persians later conquered the Babylonians. During this time, Jeremiah continued to speak and teach and love God's people and to give them hope even in the time of judgment.

Jeremiah prophesies the restoration of Judah in due time when he declares,

"The days are coming," declares the LORD,
    "when I will make a new covenant
with the people of Israel
    and with the people of Judah.
It will not be like the covenant
    I made with their ancestors
when I took them by the hand
    to lead them out of Egypt,

because they broke my covenant,
  though I was a husband to them,"
    declares the LORD.
"This is the covenant I will make with the people of Israel
  after that time," declares the LORD.
"I will put my law in their minds
  and write it on their hearts.
I will be their God,
  and they will be my people.
No longer will they teach their neighbor,
  or say to one another, 'Know the LORD,'
because they will all know me,
  from the least of them to the greatest,"
    declares the LORD.
"For I will forgive their wickedness
  and will remember their sins no more." (Jeremiah 31:31-34)

Today, we live in the light of this fulfilled promise of Jeremiah. The day has come because the Son has been glorified (John 14:15-21; 16:7-15) and the Holy Spirit, eternally proceeding from the Father and the Son, is poured out on God's people (Acts 2; 8; 10). With the real presence of the Spirit as the new Immanuel (God with us), Christians participate in the life of the true vine and bear fruit that lasts.

The Ancient Story and Our Story

If the Upper Room Discourse is a crash course in the Lord's curriculum for discipleship, this teaching on love and how Jesus modeled this on the night he was betrayed is the centerpiece of what life looks like when we "remain" intimately dependent on his life as our own. No wonder Jesus says that how we love each other is the most powerful witness of the church in the world. "By this everyone will know that you are my disciples, if you love one another" (John 13:35). Jesus loved his disciples by telling them the truth even when it was hard to hear and to "remain" in this word, commanding them to follow his example and to obey his commands, praying for them fervently and humbly, preparing them to expect both the trials and suffering to come, and promising the presence of the Holy Spirit to accompany them on life's journey. In all of this, "having loved his own who were in the world, he loved them to the end" (John 13:1).

The Scripture is full of this laying aside one's life for the sake of another—not just in "no greater love" in dying for another but in laying aside one's self in the everyday servanthood of life. Abraham laid aside his homeland (Genesis 12:1-4). Moses laid aside the riches of Egypt (Hebrews 11:24-25). Hannah laid aside her motherhood (1 Samuel 1:1–2:11). David laid aside his plans (2 Samuel 7). Isaiah laid aside his hope for a "successful" ministry (Isaiah 6). Hosea laid aside the path to a "normal" marriage. Matthew laid aside a financially comfortable job. John, Andrew and Peter laid aside their livelihood by the Sea of Galilee. Paul laid aside his religious pride (Philippians 3:4-11). And the list goes on until the kingdom comes.

The connection between the *ancient story* and *our story* is hardwired into the call of discipleship. This is because the ancient story *is* our story. To lay aside our crown for a cross or our tailored lives for a towel—this is discipleship. This is love. This is to keep Jesus' commandments, to abide in his word, to remain attached to the true vine as a fruitful branch, to be pruned to bear more fruit, to obey and believe, to believe and obey, to pray like Jesus would, to rest in his calling and work in his world.

Looking Ahead

Jesus the Son, incarnate in human flesh, had to suffer, die, rise and ascend to be glorified so that with the Father, the Spirit could abide in and remain with God's people (the Spirit proceeds from both Father and Son; see John 14:16; 16:15). The hope of disciples, like branches remaining faithfully and fruitfully in the true vine, is only ultimately possible because of the obedience and love of the Son in our place, in our flesh. The incarnation of God in Jesus Christ is the centerpiece of God's great love for the world.

Going Deeper

A concise but excellent short commentary on the Upper Room Discourse is *The Farewell Discourse and Final Prayer of Jesus: An Exposition of John 14–17* by D. A. Carson.

5 / Jesus, the Incarnate and Risen Savior

MEMORY VERSE: Luke 24:46-47
BIBLE STUDY: Luke 24:13-49
READING: The Savior of the World, the Incarnation of God

The salvation of God through the incarnation, suffering, death, resurrection and ascension of Jesus is the central story of the New Testament. Jesus' victory over sin, death and the devil is the ultimate and costly self-giving of God in Christ for the cosmos "God so loved." This victory through what seemed like defeat was a big surprise to those who had seen Jesus die. The weakness, failure and death of Jesus must have seemed like the end of the story for those who had put their hope in him.

 ## Bible Study Guide

After reading Luke 24:13-49, spend some time reflecting on it with the following questions in mind before looking at the Reading.

1. What are the day and time connections between verses 13 and 22 of the reading and Luke 24:1?

2. Luke 24:1-12 is the context for the focus reading in this study. Who are the characters and what are they doing?

3. How does the text summarize their lack of recognition in verse 16?

4. What does Cleopas's reply to Jesus in verse 18 indicate about the notoriety of the crucifixion during the Passover festival?

5. In verses 19-24, note the details and sequence of how the two disciples summarize who Jesus was, what he did and the events of the last few days. What might the mention of "the third day" (v. 21) indicate about the disciples' knowledge of Jesus' prophecy concerning the outcome of his suffering (see Luke 9:22; 13:32; 18:33; 24:7 for this pattern in the sayings of Jesus)?

6. What is the response of Jesus to the disciples in verses 25-27?

7. The practice of hospitality to strangers was highly valued in the cultures of the Near and Middle East. What is it about how Jesus, as an honored guest at the family meal, functioned as the host (v. 30) that led to the recognition of the Savior (v. 31)?

How might seeing Jesus' hands as he broke and gave them bread factor into suddenly recognizing Jesus (note v. 39 in this regard)?

8. Probably walking at a faster pace than their earlier journey to Emmaus, what do the two disciples from Emmaus discover upon their return to where the disciples were gathered in Jerusalem (v. 34)?

9. What does Jesus say and do in the presence of the disciples in verses 36-43 to "prove" to them that his is a bodily resurrection?

10. What is the explicit foundation of Jesus' teaching and the key to the disciples' understanding in verses 44-47?

🕮 Reading: The Savior of the World, the Incarnation of God

At least once a semester I will ask college students during a class to name the two books in the New Testament where they can find the term *antichrist*. They name a variety of books, but one is always the Revelation of Jesus Christ to John, the last book of the New Testament. They are surprised to be wrong. (I also tell them someday in a trivia contest, like *Jeopardy!*, they will know the right answer [or question] and win a lot of money, and that I want a tithe, but I digress.) The only two books in the New Testament that mention the antichrist are the first and second epistles of John. And in these two books the term has a precise focus and very clear delineation of what it means to stand against the Christ, the Messiah, the anointed One of God.

John makes it very clear that "many antichrists have come" (1 John 2:18) and any denial that "Christ has come in the flesh" is, in fact, the spirit of the antichrist that is "already in the world" (1 John 4:2-3). 2 John 7 makes this same point succinctly, "I say this because many deceivers, who do not acknowledge Jesus Christ as coming in the flesh, have gone out into the world. Any such person is the deceiver and the antichrist." The affirmation of the incarnation of God in Jesus Christ is a nonnegotiable centerpiece of the Christian faith.

This affirmation and confidence wasn't just vitally important for John, whose New Testament writings were first addressed to the "second generation" of the church living near the end of the first century, but to the first eyewitness accounts of Jesus' earthly life found in the Gospels and Acts, and the apostolic letters of the New Testament. The importance of affirming the reality of the incarnation of God in Christ Jesus was of particular importance to John because he was writing people who had never seen, touched or heard Jesus "in the flesh." People like us! However, as the passage for this chapter makes clear, the reality of the incarnation was the key to understanding who Jesus was, what he accomplished and who he continued to be as the Savior of the world and the Head of the church. The incarnation of God in the womb of the virgin by the overshadowing of the Spirit was and is a continuing reality after the resurrection.

This reality, however, was as unexpected as it was important to the disciples who first followed Jesus and put their hope in him. One of the great affirmations of the bodily resurrection of Jesus is the honest portrayal in all four Gospels that exposes how "slow to believe" (Luke 24:25) Jesus' disciples proved to be. The resurrection of Jesus is not an event cooked up by the early church to save face or sustain the community. If you were to make up a story in the midst of first-century Judaism, you would not record that women were the first witnesses to the empty tomb and the angelic announcement, because women had no status as dependable witnesses in everyday events, let alone official trials or legal papers. This is reflected in Luke's text when he wrote, "But they did not believe the women, because their words seemed to them like nonsense" (Luke 24:11). The incarnation and bodily resurrection of Jesus are of central importance to Christian faith, not just because the claims of the faith are grounded in real history through the documents that reliably bear witness to this history, but because the particularity of the incarnation in Jesus of Nazareth who suffered, not metaphorically but "under Pontius Pilate" as the creed states, is the bedrock of Christian witness, worship and the very mission of the church in the real world.

Notice again the detail and particularity of the story in Luke concerning the disciples. Luke notes the distance between Jerusalem and the small village of Emmaus is nearly seven miles. Biblical geographers and archaeologists affirm the the incredible accuracy of distances mentioned in biblical texts due to the many times people walked from place to place. The companion of Cleopas (v. 18) is never named and was probably his wife. Luke notes the detail of their demeanor and their discussion as they journeyed back home (vv. 14, 17). Luke makes the appearance of Jesus in the story emphatic (v. 15). Equally emphatic language will be repeated by Jesus himself when he appears later in Jerusalem (v. 39).

Jesus first joins the two disciples on a real road where Luke notes that they were so surprised by the cluelessness of the stranger who joins them that "they stood still, their faces downcast" (v. 17). The concern of Cleopas and his companion (probably his wife, who would have spoken to the women who had come from the tomb with some intimacy) was centered around the fact that the women bearing spices for the burial shroud "didn't find his body" (Luke 24:2, 23) and that other disciples who went to check out what the women said "found it just as the women said, but they did not see Jesus" (Luke 24:24). The importance of seeing in order to believe is not just for people from Missouri, the "Show Me!" state, but for these people who had seen the Lord flogged, beaten, spit upon, stripped, mocked, impaled with thorns and finally tortured to the point of being too physically weak to carry his own crossbeam for his execution. Some of these eyewitnesses stayed at the "place called the Skull" (Luke 23:33) and witnessed the crucifixion and death of Jesus (Luke 23:49). People in the first century were not isolated from death, as many of us are—they knew what death looked like in their homes, they washed the dead, they knew what cold, bluish mottled skin looked like and felt like. On that first Good Friday, people handled the dead, breathless and bruised body of Jesus when a man from Arimathea "took it down, wrapped it in linen cloth and placed it in a tomb cut in the rock, one in which no one had yet been laid," just before the sun set as the sabbath day was about to begin (Luke 23:53-54). Jesus was dead, not breathing, cold, wounds no longer bleeding, still, silent, gone, just like any other beloved human being they had to prepare for burial and mourn.

No wonder the two walking to Emmaus

had downcast faces. No wonder they were "slow to believe." No wonder they only began to believe when they saw Jesus' hands in the breaking of the bread, when in Jerusalem they saw his flesh and bones and wounds (Luke 24:37-40; John 20:19-20, 24-28). No wonder Jesus had to break through their incredulity by taking a piece of fish and eating it in front of them (Luke 24:41-43) to try and prove to them he was really bodily alive and there with them! In a sense all the disciples had to go through the transformation that Cleopas and his companion did—from eyes that could not recognize the Lord (Luke 24:16) to eyes being opened to recognize him (v. 31), to the opening of their minds so they could understand the Scriptures (v. 45) that they had heard before, but did not comprehend.

Luke, of course, continues this story in Acts 1 in greater detail regarding the Lord's ascension after forty days, and in Acts 2:9-10 mentions the people like these two disciples present at the festival in Jerusalem. For Jews living outside of Palestine the opportunity to celebrate Passover in Jerusalem was often a once-in-a-lifetime experience. Since the trip was costly and time consuming, pilgrims would often arrive before Passover and stay through the festival of Pentecost, approximately fifty days later. The other Gospel writers tell other stories of Jesus' appearances from Jerusalem to Galilee, and the apostle Paul, in his famous chapter on the resurrection of the body, relates the stories he had received by both the Spirit and the apostles concerning the postresurrection appearances of Jesus—even to "more than five hundred of the brothers and sisters at the same time, most of whom are still living" (1 Corinthians 15:3-7). Beyond this, Luke reminds his readers that what these first disciples went through was then (and still is!) the reality of the church. The disciples of Emmaus recognized Jesus and then "he disappeared from their sight" (Luke 24:31) and again after the appearing in Jerusalem, in the "vicinity of Bethany. . . . While he was blessing them, he left them" (vv. 50-51). Ever since that moment, believers have been challenged to believe in the incarnate, risen and ascended Jesus through this apostolic witness, fully by faith and not by sight. John's Gospel records the importance of this ongoing dynamic in the words of Jesus himself, "Because you have seen me, you have believed; blessed are those who have not seen and yet have believed" (John 20:29). This is the faith demanded and blessing given for those who have received the grace to believe to this very day. Paul warns, "If there is no resurrection of the dead, then not even Christ has been raised. And if Christ has not been raised, our preaching is useless and so is your faith. More than that, we are then found to be false witnesses about God, for we have testified about God that he raised Christ from the dead" (1 Corinthians 15:13-15).

Reading Study Guide

1. What can you do to make Scripture study a more significant part of your regular schedule?

   Ask someone, a friend, prayer partner, pastor or family member, to help you think through the time it would take, the resources that may be helpful and the need for graceful accountability to make progress for a renewed commitment to learning more from God's Word.

2. Think about how you tend to speak about Jesus to others. How much of what you say is grounded in the story of Scripture and how much is more a reflection of your own story or experience?

   How do you think about or visualize God the Father and Jesus the Son while you pray as a part of this reflection?

3. Take a week to read through the passion narratives (the accounts of Jesus' arrest, trials, harsh treatment and crucifixion), and the accounts of the resurrection, in all four Gospels (Matthew 26:14–28:10; Mark 14:27–16:8; Luke 22:47–24:12; John 18:2–20:18). As you read, place yourself as an intimate spectator watching this beloved rabbi and consider what it might have been like to be there: What would you have felt? What would have been confusing? What questions you would want to ask?

4. Talk to leaders in your congregation and find out about different opportunities to participate in Bible studies as a part of your faith community. How can you be equipped to lead or continue to lead a Bible study for others?

What Scripture studies in your congregation are offered for children and youth?

5. Since the embodiment of "doing the word" and not just hearing it is important in the New Testament (Matthew 7:24-27; 25:34-40; James 2:15-19; 1 John 3:16-18), what are some specific ways to connect your study of the Scripture, or that of your Bible study group, with the doing of the Word? For example: hands-on mission, some sort of outreach or service to those with needs in the congregation and so forth.

6. J. I. Packer, in his book *Knowing God*, focuses on the significance of the incarnation as God's "greatest mystery":

"Tis mystery all! The immortal dies," wrote Wesley; but there is no comparable mystery in the Immortal's resurrection. And if the immortal Son of God did really submit to taste death, it is not strange that such a death should have saving significance for a doomed race. Once we grant that Jesus was divine, it becomes unreasonable to find difficulty in any of this; it is all of a piece and hangs together completely. The Incarnation is in itself an unfathomable mystery, but it makes sense of everything else that the New Testament contains.[*]

Read through the stories of Jesus' birth in Luke and Matthew and meditate on the significance of affirming by faith this central tenant of the Christian faith that John summarizes beautifully when he writes.

---

[*]J. I. Packer, *Knowing God* (Downers Grove, IL: InterVarsity Press, 1993), p. 54.

The Word became flesh and made his dwelling among us. We have seen his glory, the glory of the one and only Son, who came from the Father, full of grace and truth. . . . No one has ever seen God, but the one and only Son, who is himself God and is in closest relationship with the Father, has made him known (John 1:14, 18).

➡ Connecting to the Old Testament

The seduction into sin began with the tempter saying, "Did God really say . . . ?" (Genesis 3:1). The descent into sin continued as the woman embellished God's word (given in Genesis 2:17) and tweaked the prohibition by adding to it (Genesis 3:3). Casting doubt on the truthfulness of God's word or misrepresenting and misunderstanding God's word (even with the best of intentions) is literally as old as Eden. The knowledge of good and evil was always intended to be mediated by God's person and his holiness, integrity and perfect judgment. Whenever anyone defines good and evil on their own, apart from the mediation of God's word and wisdom and person, this is the genesis of all sin and rebellion in the biblical account and in our own lives.

Thus, the flip side of this sad coin—believing and obeying God's word—is the hallmark of people who please God and are blessed by God. Abraham heard God say, "Go" and he went (Genesis 12:1-4). Abraham believed God's promise concerning his need for an heir, and even in the face of what seemed impossible, "Abraham believed the LORD, and [the Lord] credited it to him as righteousness" (Genesis 15:6). This verse in Genesis becomes the basis for Paul's explanation (in all thirteen of his letters in the New Testament, particularly notable in Galatians and Romans) of how righteousness comes by faith in God alone, not by genealogy or the perfection of self-generated and self-dependent attempts to be holy. Believing God's word and acting on this belief by faith through grace is in large measure a summary of the salvation and sanctification of the Christian. Both salvation and sanctification are works of God's grace and both are defined and illustrated in the Word of God, the Scriptures of the Old and New Testaments.

To know Jesus and to recognize him through the work of the Spirit in the church and in the world today, God's people must be students of God's Word, learning "what was said in all the Scriptures" (Luke 24:27). As students of the Word, "clothed with power from on high" by the Holy Spirit, we can teach and preach the Word of God, and bear truthful witness to what God has done and how God has made himself known throughout the world in Jesus the incarnate Son (Luke 24:45-49).

💬 The Ancient Story and Our Story

Jesus is the Savior of the world because of who he is and what he did as the incarnate Son of God in his coming, suffering, dying, rising and ascending. The affirmation of the incarnation of God the Son is the foundational confession of the church that defines the Christian faith and is the reason for the real embodiment of Christian mission and worship. Because of the incarnation it is not enough to *feel* badly about people going hungry; Christians must feed the hungry. Because of the incarnation we can't just *say* we love each other; we have to serve each other concretely and bear one another's burdens sacrificially. Because of the incarnation Christian worship is meant to be a reenactment of the story of salvation from beginning to end, from call to benediction. The Christian life is all about "this same Jesus" (Acts 1:11), whom the disciples from the beginning heard, saw with their eyes and touched with their hands—this Jesus is "the Word of life" (1 John 1:1-4).

"This same Jesus" can only be truly known through the Scriptures of the New Testament. This speaks to the particularity of the incarnation—God didn't just become any man, but God was incarnate in the womb of a virgin who was engaged to a godly man from the tribe of Judah. Jesus grew up in a Galilean city on a Palestinian trade route in the Roman Empire during the reign of Caesar Augustus. Christians must know "this Jesus" the same way these first disciples began to know who Jesus was—through the Scriptures of the Old and New Testaments. Over and over again in the Gospels and the rest of the New Testament Jesus is tied in a myriad of ways to the prophecies and teachings of the Old Testament. In Luke 24, the passage that is the focus of this chapter, both the disciples on the road to Emmaus and those in Jerusalem begin to understand who this risen Savior is as Jesus taught them the Scriptures.

I've participated in many Bible studies in my years as a disciple, but to have tagged along on that road to Emmaus and heard Jesus when "beginning with Moses and all the Prophets, he explained to them what was said in all the Scriptures concerning himself"—well, no wonder they invited him to stay for dinner and keep talking! When their eyes were opened, the two disciples "asked each other, 'Were not our hearts burning within us while he talked with us on the road and opened the Scriptures to us?'" (Luke 24:32). In Jerusalem Jesus focuses on the importance of knowing God's Word in order to understand who he is and what he had to do. Jesus reminds them,

> "This is what I told you while I was still with you: Everything must be fulfilled that is written about me in the Law of Moses, the Prophets and the Psalms." Then he opened their minds so they could understand the Scriptures. He told them, "This is what is written: The Messiah will suffer and rise from the dead on the third day." (Luke 24:44-46)

Part of the reason the disciples were so "slow to believe" was that they expected a Messiah of their own imaginations, born out of their own needs and situation. It is very easy for Christians today to fall into this same pattern of making Jesus into our own image. And we end up with an imaginary Jesus who can meet our needs and soothe our souls and make everything better. This makes the gospel into nothing but a religious self-help program. The Scripture confronts our penchant for separating discipleship from suffering, just like first-century disciples separated the Messiah from the suffering (Luke 24:26, 46-47). Scripture is the only authority for Christian faith and practice. It is in the Scripture that, by the illuminating power of the Spirit, we grow to understand that the way to glory is the way of the cross, the narrow way that leads to life. To be a disciple today is to be a lifelong student of the Scripture.

Looking Ahead

Only when the disciples were "clothed with power from on high" (Luke 24:49) were they enabled to truly understand who Jesus was, what he had accomplished and begin to fulfill the commission they had received from Jesus to herald the inauguration of God's kingdom and the eternal reign of God's anointed One, his beloved Son. The sending of God's Spirit to empower the church for its witness and work in the world is the focus of the rest of the New Testament.

Going Deeper

For a book that reflects beautifully on the person of Jesus Christ, read John Stott's *The Incomparable Christ* (InterVarsity Press, 2001). The four parts of the book are titled "The Original Jesus: How the New Testament Witnesses to Him," "The Ecclesiastical Jesus: How the Church Has Presented Him," "The Influential Jesus: How He Has Inspired People" and "The Eternal Jesus: How He Challenges Us Today."

Part Two

THE INDWELLING OF GOD IN THE CHURCH BY THE HOLY SPIRIT

6 / The Spirit as the New Emmanuel

LOOKING AHEAD

MEMORY VERSE: Acts 1:8
BIBLE STUDY: Acts 1:3-8; 2:1-18, 22-25, 32-41
READING: Becoming an Eyewitness to the Good News

The outpouring of God's Spirit on the church in the book of Acts is the empowerment of God's people for witness, work and worship in the world. The fruit of the Spirit and the gifts of the Spirit for the church are the identifying marks of God's people as they faithfully embody the real presence of God in the world.

 ## Bible Study Guide

After reading Acts 1:3-8; 2:1-18, 22-25, 32-41, spend some time reflecting on it with the following questions in mind before looking at the Reading.

1. The book of Acts is the second of a two-volume work written by Luke. Read the ending of Luke's Gospel (Luke 24:45-53) and then read Acts 1:1-9. How do these two passages overlap?

2. The account of the disciples from Emmaus (Luke 24:13-35) is a part of the time period between Jesus' resurrection and ascension that Luke summarizes in Acts 1:3. What is the setting and the command and promise of Jesus in Acts 1:4-5?

3. What does Acts 1:6 indicate about the disciple's expectations at this time concerning Jesus' command and promise?

How does the disciples' question in Acts 1:6 relate to their concern at Caesarea Philippi in Mark 8:27-33 and the disciples of Emmaus in Luke 24:18-21?

How does Jesus' reply to the disciples' question (Acts 1:7-8) begin to redefine and anticipate the continuing manifestation of God's kingdom that will commence with the inauguration of the Spirit's promised outpouring on Jesus' followers?

4. Approximately ten days after the bodily ascension of Jesus (Acts 1:9), the promise of Jesus is fulfilled for the disciples. What does Luke emphasize concerning the ascension in Acts 1:9-11?

What are the main points of Luke's description of the event of the Spirit's outpouring on the Day of Pentecost recorded in Acts 2:1-4?

5. The "tongues" (vv. 4, 6, 11) were languages known to the pilgrims who saw and heard those who had been filled by the Holy Spirit. How does Luke summarize the variety of responses to this surprising phenomenon (vv. 12-13)? (See also Peter's protest in Acts 2:15.)

6. How is Peter's first sermon (vv. 14-36) a fulfillment of Jesus' promise in Acts 1:8? What emphasis is made by the repetition of "this Jesus" in Acts 2:32, 36 (also a similar expression in verse 23)?

7. What is the response of the people to Peter's sermon (v. 37)?

How did Peter reply and continue to interact with the crowd (vv. 38-41)?

8. Acts 1:8 is actually the geographical outline for the entire book of Acts as the gospel spreads from Jerusalem through Judea (chaps. 1–7), to Samaria (chap. 8) and throughout the empire (Acts 13–28). It is also important to note that Peter is the only one of the original disciples to witness the Spirit's outpouring on three distinct ethnic groups: the Jews at Pentecost (Acts 2), the Samaritans (Acts 8:14-17) and finally the non-Semites, the Gentiles (Acts 10). How does the book of Acts relate to the following:
- the prophecy of Jesus concerning Peter in Matthew 16:15-19?

- the commissioning of the disciples in Matthew 28:18-20?

- the answer to Jesus' prayer in John 17:20-23?

👓 Reading: Becoming an Eyewitness to the Good News

It's not unusual for Christians to wonder from time to time what it would have been like to be a disciple of Jesus during the time of his earthly ministry. What did Jesus look like? How did his voice sound? We wonder how exciting it would have been to have witnessed one of Jesus' miracles or to have heard the Sermon on the Mount then and there. Along with these musings we can also shake our heads and wonder too how so many people didn't believe him, didn't accept him—how many people dismissed his claims and denied his identity. And, too often, we want to think better of ourselves. If *we* had been there, surely *we* would have known the truth, understood his ministry, anticipated his kingdom rightly and believed in Jesus.

But isn't it astounding that even after the resurrection—even after Jesus' postresurrection teachings, clarifications and physical proofs, including watching Jesus eat for nearly a month and a half—even after all this, the disciples are still looking for the Messiah of their own expectations. The disciples still long for the vindication of Israel as an earthy kingdom and secure political power. It's very clear in the New Testament that none of the disciples really got it—they still asked the wrong question (Acts 1:6). Prior to the outpouring of God's Spirit beginning at Pentecost—apart from the insight only the Holy Spirit would give—they were simply limited to their own best ideas. Apart from the Holy Spirit, even the disciples had to settle for what their own efforts could accomplish to do what was right. Peter's leadership was certainly marked by restraint and kindness concerning the betrayal and subsequent death of Judas (see Acts 1:15-17). The disciples wisely came to the conclusion that only a person who was an eyewitness to the whole of Jesus' ministry could replace Judas (Acts 1:20-23), but even after a time of prayer, they were left to the basic Jewish confidence in God's ultimate sovereignty through the practice of casting lots. Without the inner discernment of God's Spirit, Matthias was elected essentially to the near equivalent of a coin flip or the drawing of straws.

And then "suddenly" (Acts 2:2) the Spirit promised by Jesus (John 15:26–16:15) was sent from the Father and the Son, and nothing has ever been the same. The Spirit who had been given in the Old Testament to prophets for a particular word or a ruler for a particular task was now unleashed in the world because the work of the Son was finished and Jesus was now glorified. Starting with the first Jewish disciples (Acts 2) and those pilgrims in Jerusalem, extending to their long lost and much despised Semitic cousins in Samaria (Acts 8) and then, as the biggest surprise of all, falling on the unwashed and uncircumcised Gentiles (Acts 10), the Spirit, as an act of new creation, gave birth to the church of Jesus Christ. The Holy Spirit is the new Immanuel, God with us! As much as we like to daydream about what it would have been like to follow Jesus on the dusty roads of Galilee, there is no comparison to what it means to live by the Spirit in the world God wants us to love and serve today. The reality of belonging in the Father's house through the mediation of God's Son by the power of God's Spirit is the supreme wonder of wonders. The life of the church should be marked by unexplainable relationships and the power of an undeniable love for each other, the world and even the enemies of the church.

Only by the Spirit is our journey toward the kingdom both joyful and steadfast. The community of the church, not defined by ethnic identity, socioeconomic status or one's gender (Galatians 3:26-29), is the fullest expression of what it means to bear the image of God in the world. To live as a child of God, inhabited by God's Spirit, who continues dynamically to proceed from the Father and the Son into our lives, is to participate in "the church, which is his body, the fullness of him who fills everything in every way" (Ephesians 1:22-23) in order to be witnesses to Christ Jesus in the world. From God's perspective the church is not a means to some other ends. By the Spirit, the church is God's ultimate point. The salvation of the world has been accomplished in the incarnation, life, death, resurrection and ascension of Jesus. The tomb is empty, the Spirit is poured out and the kingdom will come in its fullness in the day of the Lord. This is the story we tell the world and demonstrate with our lives. For this witness, the Spirit has come with power.

Reading Study Guide

1. How do you discern the work of the Spirit in everyday life?

2. Think about a time when you have experienced the Holy Spirit's work in your life in a particular or surprising way or in a specific situation. Write a short summary of this experience and then consider how it might relate to an experience of someone in the Scripture.

3. What, generally, is the way the Holy Spirit relates most prominently to your congregation or other faith community?

   How is the presence and work of the Holy Spirit explained in this community by those in leadership?

4. One predominant work of the Holy Spirit in the New Testament was that of building unexplainable unity out of very diverse people (like the Jews and Greeks, slaves and free, men and women in Galatians 3:27-28). What surprising unity is apparent in your congregation that gives unexplainable evidence of this work of God's Spirit?

How might this become even a greater manifestation of God's good work in your faith community?

5. It's not uncommon for Christians to think about the Holy Spirit as either an impersonal power of God or something just left behind by God until Jesus comes again. Sometimes we get these ideas through song and hymn lyrics that have been unmoored from the Scripture! Read through the lyrics of church music that are fairly common in your services of worship. How is the eternal sending of the Holy Spirit on the church reflected (or not) in some of the lyrics?

6. Christmas and Easter are creatively and consistently celebrated by most congregations. How does your faith community remember the ascension or Pentecost?

Find a calendar for the liturgical year in a book or on the Internet and work with worship or church education leaders to celebrate the whole story of Jesus in the coming year.

7. The Spirit of God gives gifts, bears fruit and yields the character of God in those in whom
   he dwells. Read the following passages in the New Testament that speak of the character,
   gifts and fruit of the Spirit. Write what you have learned from each.

   • 1 Corinthians 12:4-11

   • 1 Corinthians 13

   • 1 Corinthians 14:1-25

   • Ephesians 4:1-7

   • Ephesians 4:11-16

   • Galatians 5:22-26

   • Colossians 3:12-17

   • Romans 12:3-8

8. For several weeks, months or a year, keep a journal that helps you focus on discerning the work of God by the Spirit of Christ Jesus in and through your life. After the set length of time, read back through the journal and consider how the Spirit has been faithful to mature your faith, develop your spiritual gifts and bear God's fruit as a disciple.

Connecting to the Old Testament

The signs of the Spirit's outpouring: mighty wind, the sight of small flames on one's head and the sudden change of human language or ability all have echoes of God's presence in the Old Testament (Joel 2:28-32). First, the Hebrew word for "spirit" is the same as that for "wind" or "breath." The "Spirit of God" present before the first act of creation (Genesis 1:2) is the same word used when the Lord God, Yahweh, "breathed" into the nostrils of the man he had formed from the dust of the ground (Genesis 2:7). John's Gospel carries the idea of re-creation of the new humanity when he writes, "[Jesus] breathed on them and said, 'Receive the Holy Spirit'" (John 20:22). Though his Gospel was written about fifty years after the event, the writer of the fourth Gospel was well aware of what happened in Jerusalem on the first Pentecost. And Luke's two-volume work was in circulation for nearly thirty years by the time John, as the last apostolic eyewitness, wrote his account early in the last decade of the first century. John's Gospel also includes the unique account of Jesus' encounter with Nicodemus, when he explains the work of the Spirit with the metaphor of wind. On that night Jesus explained the surprising and uncontrollable work of God's Spirit by saying to Nicodemus, "The wind blows wherever it pleases. You hear its sound, but you cannot tell where it comes from or where it is going. So it is with everyone born of the Spirit" (John 3:8). Certainly, God's Spirit is not indicated every time the word *wind* is mentioned in the Old Testament, but there are more than a few times in the Psalms (see Psalm 104:4, for example) and the Prophets (like Ezekiel 37:9) that the wind as the breath of God accomplishes his life-giving will.

The presence of God's Spirit appearing like small flames in the Old Testament is a bit more rare, but these appearances lend great insight regarding this manifestation over the heads of the gathered disciples at Pentecost (see Psalm 104:4 for this metaphor again!). Isaiah 6:2, 6, is the only mention of "seraphim" in the Hebrew Scripture. The literal meaning of the Hebrew word is "fiery or burning ones." These flames, which flew with multiple wings and cried "Holy, Holy, Holy" in heavenly worship are the same as those who took the coal from the altar to touch Isaiah's mouth as a cleansing and gifting preparation for his ministry. The word Luke uses in Acts 2 translated "tongues of fire" is the identical word used in the Greek translation of the Old Testament (LXX, the Septuagint) for "seraphim"! Like Isaiah the disciples at Pentecost were baptized by the cleansing gift of holy fire to prepare them for ministry.

Last, the gift of the disciples witnessing to the crowd that gathered in Jerusalem in languages they had never learned is, literally, the reversal of what occurred as a result of God's judgment for the pride and ambition of humanity that culminated in building the Tower of Babel (Genesis 11:1-9). The undoing of "babbling" at Pentecost was designed to herald the unity of God's people founded not upon human pride and power but upon the humiliation of the crucified Messiah of God. In the church of Jesus Christ, God's "weakness" and "foolishness" would prove to be greater than any scheme of humankind to achieve the "power" and "wisdom" of its own making (1 Corinthians 1:18-31).

When the Spirit was poured out on the disciples in Jerusalem on Pentecost, the Festival of Harvest (Exodus 23:16), it was a surprise for everyone but the triune God of grace. The Father, Son and Spirit had been at work on this gift since the beginning of the story itself.

◐ The Ancient Story and Our Story

The Nicene-Constantinople Creed of the early church summarizes what is taught in the Scriptures, and in doing so describes the person of the Holy Spirit as "the Lord and Giver of Life." The Spirit, as Paul writes in Ephesians, is the divine "seal" of God's promise, the "deposit guaranteeing our inheritance until the redemption of those who are God's possession—to the praise of his glory" (Ephesians 1:13-14).

In fact, in the incarnation Jesus was utterly dependent on the Holy Spirit for his guidance, obedience and wisdom. Probably because he was writing mostly to Gentiles and also anticipating the coming of the Spirit on the church in volume two of his work, Luke's Gospel makes Jesus' dependence on and awareness of the Spirit very explicit. "Jesus, full of the Holy Spirit, left the Jordan" (Luke 4:1) and "Jesus returned to Galilee in the power of the Spirit" (Luke 4:14) are just two examples of this.

To be increasingly conscious of the need for spiritual "ears to hear" (Mark 4:23; Luke 8:8; 14:35) is important for the Christian to mature in faith and obedience. The Spirit is the dynamic reality of abiding in Christ, as the Spirit of Christ abides in us. To abide in God's Word, to spend time in reading and studying the Scripture, is one way to become more aware of who the Spirit is and what he does in each believer and in and through the body of Christ.

Peter's sermon in Acts 2 is a *pesher*, an ancient story (Peter's use of Joel's prophecy) understood in the light of a contemporary reality (the outpouring of the Spirit on the gathered community of believers at Pentecost—about 120 people according to Acts 1:15!). Speeches in Acts are exceptionally prevalent. In fact, the nineteen speeches in Acts comprise about 25 percent of the entire book. This makes sense because Luke's first reader,

Theophilus (Luke 1:3-4; Acts 1:1), and by extension his Gentile (non-Jewish) friends and family, would need extra help in learning the story of Israel and its God, and then in connecting this to the story of Jesus and the gospel. The Christian faith cannot lose its Jewish accent, because the work of Jesus fulfilled the law with surpassing righteousness and fulfilled all the messianic hopes that the prophets foretold (Matthew 5:17; John 1:45).

LOOKING AHEAD

In study 7, we will consider the unity of the church. The unity of believers by the Spirit is the deepest work of God since Pentecost, the work God most longs to see come to completion in the body of Christ. This supreme work of God is also the hardest for us to experience. Scripture has much to teach us about what it means to love one another the way God does.

Going Deeper

A good Bible atlas is the next best thing to taking an extensive trip to the Middle East and the Mediterranean world. It's quite helpful to have one at hand while reading Acts and following the expansion of the church and the missionary journeys of the apostles. I recommend the *Zondervan NIV Atlas of the Bible*, edited by Carl Rasmussen. It is as affordable as it is helpful!

7 / The Church as the Body of Christ

LOOKING AHEAD

MEMORY VERSE: Ephesians 4:4-6
BIBLE STUDY: Ephesians 2:11–3:6
READING: The Body of Christ, the Mystery of the Gospel Unveiled

The headship of Christ Jesus, which unifies the church as his body, is a major theme in the New Testament. The singular headship of Christ leads the church to acknowledge this unity in Christ through the proclamation of the gospel, which is based on the witness of the apostles and the authority of Scripture, and through the demonstration of this same good news in mission as the body of Christ doing the work of God in the world in the power of the Spirit.

 ## Bible Study Guide

After reading Ephesians 2:11–3:6, spend some time reflecting on it with the following questions in mind before looking at the Reading.

1. Read the immediate context for this study's passage (Ephesians 2:1-10) and note how Paul summarizes salvation by grace (vv. 5, 8) as God's love (v. 4) for those "dead in transgressions and sins" (v. 1) whom God "made alive" (v. 5) and "raised up" (v. 6) on the basis of faith alone (vv. 8-9). What connections do you find between this summary introduction in chapter 2 and the teaching Paul continues in verses 11-22?

2. What is the main point in verses 11-12 indicated by the repetition of the word *remember*?

Who are the "circumcised" and "uncircumcised" Paul addresses?

What are the five significant deficits, delineated by Paul, that the Gentiles faced before salvation (v. 12)?

3. Note in verse 13 how the solution for the dilemma of the Gentiles is stated very similarly to the dynamics of salvation in verse 5. How is God as the source and initiator of salvation made clear in Paul's argument?

4. In verses 14-18 Paul is explicit about what Christ Jesus has done to reconcile both Jews and Gentiles to each other and to God. What points does Paul make about this central work of divine reconciliation?

5. Note Paul's central claim concerning peace in verse 14 and how this counters any notion that peace is not the result of an agreement or the cessation of hostilities between two factions. With this in mind, count how many times the idea of "in Christ" (or "in him," "with him," "through Christ," etc.) occurs in the passage for this study (include verses 1-10 if you have time). How is this significant to the Christian life?

6. *Shalom* is the Hebrew word that carries the broad sense of the fullness of well-being. "Paul's predominant use of the word in Ephesians is connected to the idea of the sinners' peace with God and the believers' peace with one another"* The word *peace* (reflective

of the Hebrew word *shalom* in Paul's understanding and use) occurs four times in verses 14-18. What are the specific ways the word is used in each instance?

7. Note the word *one* in verses 14-18, which occurs four times. How is this word used in the passage to denote a present reality for God's people and not just something to be achieved in the future?

8. Verse 19 begins with the word *consequently*, signaling the results of what Paul has been declaring. What are the consequences of what God has done through Christ Jesus by the Spirit in the conclusion of this passage (vv. 19-22)?

9. In Ephesians 3:2-13, Paul reflects on his participation as a herald of God's grace and peace concerning the reconciliation of Jews and Gentiles in Christ that he has set forth in chapter 2. Paul uses the word *mystery* (something unveiled that had been hidden) in verses 2-6 partly to indicate the surprising nature of sinners being reconciled to God, and further, the reconciliation in Christ by the Spirit of Jews and Gentiles to each other. How did Paul come to know this divine mystery that he has just explained briefly in the preceding chapter (Ephesians 3:3)?

How had the mystery first been revealed to the church (v. 5)?

How does Paul summarize the mystery in verse 6?

---

*Harold Hoehner, *Ephesians* (Grand Rapids: Baker Academic, 2002), pp. 149-50, 366-67.

Reading: The Body of Christ, the Mystery of the Gospel Unveiled

Ephesus in the first century was the fourth largest city of the Roman Empire and was like many big cities around the world today. It was a city addicted to wealth and prestige, a place where superstition marked everything from sports to sacred practices, with homes scarred by infidelity and deviant sexual practices, and a popular destination for all sorts of people who loved to mix business with pleasure, lots and lots of pleasure. The population of Ephesus also had a robust energy when it came to issues of spirituality and religion. At least seventeen deities other than the Greek fertility goddess Artemis (Diana in the Roman pantheon) were recognized in Ephesus. In addition, there was a sizable Jewish community, and it seems that at least a few influential Jews had participated in the ministry of John the Baptist with the baptism of repentance (Acts 19:1-7).

Ephesus is the social, cultural and religious backdrop for more than a few New Testament books. Church tradition has long held that John the apostle moved to Ephesus prior to the fall of Jerusalem in A.D. 70, and John's Gospel and his three epistles were probably written from Ephesus. Patmos, the island of John's exile, is just fifty miles southwest of Ephesus. The first letter in the book of the Revelation is addressed to the church at Ephesus (Revelation 2:1-7). The main base for Timothy's ministry was also in and near Ephesus,

and Paul's letters to Timothy reflect a bit of the city's challenging culture.

Paul visited Ephesus during his second missionary journey, to help establish the disciples on a firmer foundation (Acts 18:19-21). Paul returned during his third journey and stayed in the city for two years and turned the city inside out. From turmoil with some in the synagogue, to a fraudulent exorcist, to a revival that led to the burning of occult books, to a protest over the economic downturn in the sale of idols that led to a riot in the marketplace, Paul's early ministry helped establish a community of believers that had quite a witness in the city (Acts 19:8–20:1).[1] Paul deeply loved the leaders of the Ephesian congregations and his farewell to them (Acts 20:17-38) is often considered the most emotionally moving account of affection in the New Testament. When Paul wrote to the Ephesian Christians during his first imprisonment, he knew the people he wrote to and understood the challenges they faced to be the church of Jesus Christ in the city of Ephesus.

Living in a place that was openly hostile to the Christian faith caused the church in Ephesus to clearly and fervently define itself in distinction from the culture of the city. Ephesian Christians and their house-church consortia were known for their fervent and doctrinally correct biblical theology. In the letter written to the believers in Ephesus in the book of Revelation, Jesus himself commends them for their "deeds, . . . hard work and . . . perseverance." He also says "that you cannot tolerate wicked people, that you have tested those who claim to be apostles but are not, and have found them false. You have persevered and have endured hardships for my name, and have not grown weary. . . . You hate the practices of the Nicolaitans" (Revelation 2:2-3, 6). Late in the first century the Ephesian church was known for its robust defense of the gospel in the "party capital" of Asia Minor, but Jesus rebukes the church in Ephesus for its weakness, their lack of love for each other and for the Lord (Revelation 2:4). No wonder the apostle John, who lived in Ephesus when he wrote his Gospel and his pastoral letters, recalled the "new command" of Jesus so clearly! "Love one another. . . . By this everyone will know that you are my disciples, if you love one another" (John 13:34-35). In addition, John's admonition to the church in 1 John revolves around the need for one's love of God to be manifest in love for one's brothers and sisters in Christ—and this emphasis is repeated over and over again throughout this first epistle.

However, it is significant to note that a little over thirty years before John's writings, Paul in his letter to the Ephesians and in one of his letters to Timothy prophetically puts his finger on the very thing for which Jesus, in Revelation 2, chastises the Ephesian church. The struggle of the Ephesian Christians to love each other well troubled Paul deeply. The advice Paul gives the young Ephesian pastor Timothy from prison is telling. Paul reminds Timothy that the goal of teaching sound doctrine is love (1 Timothy 1:3-5). It seems, in the long run, that the Ephesians got an A-plus in doctrine, but they were failing to achieve its very goal, love itself. Through the Spirit's discernment in his life, Paul realized this was the real challenge for the Ephesian Christians. Jesus, Paul and John are convinced that the church's best witness to the world is how brothers and sisters in Christ love each other—especially brothers and sisters who have very little in common apart from their "sound doctrine" in the faith.

The problem that occupies Paul in his letter to the Ephesians is their struggle with racism. Jewish believers and Gentile believers had so little in common apart from faith in the saving work of Christ. The Ephesian believers found it much simpler to have congregations isolated from each other, denying their need for the other, and both were on the brink of thinking they could bifurcate the headship of Christ Jesus over two bodies of believers. Paul's letter to the Ephesian Christians, from beginning to end, carefully and profoundly makes it clear that this is not possible because "there is one body and one Spirit, just as you were called to one hope when you were called; one Lord, one faith, one baptism; one God and Father of all, who is over all and through all and in all" (Ephesians 4:4-6). There is not one community for Jews and another for Gentiles, nor one for slaves and another for masters, nor one for men and another for women, nor one for this culture and another for that culture, because Jesus is the Head of the one church, "which is his body, the fullness of him who fills everything in every way" (Ephesians 1:23). The unity of the church in Christ is a nonnegotiable reality of the faith, and the manifestation of this eternal and spiritual reality is not reserved for the perfection of eternal life, the "circle unbroken" only "in the sweet bye 'n bye." No, the church is the dwelling place of God by the Spirit (Ephesians 2:22) in the here and now reality of cities and places and people who need to see how good life can be when very different people love each other extravagantly. The church is not a comfort zone—it is a community of people, once foreigners and strangers, who are joined together and rise to be a holy temple, the very place where love is the supreme evidence of belonging to Christ Jesus.

---

[1]Acts 19:17-20 records that the books burned were valued at "fifty thousand drachmas." A drachma was a silver coin considered a day's wage at the time: 136 years' worth of an average salary, up in smoke!

Reading Study Guide

1. Take time to slowly read through the entire book of Ephesians and highlight the words *in Christ, in him, through Christ* and the like throughout the letter. What does this teach us about Christ as the mediator not just of salvation but of relationships within the body of Christ?

2. Read Paul's prayer in Ephesians 3:14-21, which follows our Bible study passage. Rewrite this prayer in your own words.

3. Ask someone in your congregation to join you in praying Paul's prayer for the Ephesian Christians for your community of faith. Do this daily for a week, or weekly for a month or a year.

4. Reflect on the kind of people of faith you most enjoy being with, the brothers and sisters who easily fit in your own comfort zone. What sorts of things do you hold in common?

   How are differences addressed or accommodated?

What might be a good first step for this circle of faith-sharing friends to open up to include others?

5. Reflect on the kinds of people you are generally less comfortable with or even uncomfortable to be around. What in your own life, background, experiences, upbringing, relationships, socioeconomic or educational status may account for this lack of ease or acceptance of these people, even for those who share your faith in Christ?

6. It is quite common for congregations or other faith communities to reflect a homogeneity or sameness concerning all sorts of distinctions besides ethnic identity or race. For instance congregations can reflect a certain age range, marital status, cultural preferences, socioeconomic status, educational background, physical ability or disability, or the inadvertent or deliberate inclusion or exclusion of children. Consider the subtle ways your family of faith tends to look like a comfort zone and less like a community of people working on manifesting its union in Christ. (For instance, does a preference for a certain style of music bifurcate the congregation's worship services? Does a youth group have its own worship service? Are families with children getting to know the single college students? How do the blue collar folks and the educators and executives get to know each other?)

7. Think about ways you can begin to get to know people who are different from you in terms of race, family configuration, cultural experiences, physical abilities or disabilities, age, general interests and the like. What communities of God's people distinct from your own can you join and participate with to enjoy and learn from your shared unity in Christ?

8. Read 1 John every week for a month or two and note the maturity of faith God longs for concerning how brothers and sisters love one another as an expression of their faith in the God who loved them first.

 ## Connecting to the Old Testament

The ministry to the Gentiles was greatly accelerated by Paul's missionary work, but the initial witness to the Gentiles came about in an extraordinary way through Simon Peter. This story is narrated in great detail in Acts 10:1–11:21. It took a visit by an angel of God, a series of visions and the voice of God to get very Jewish and circumcised Peter to travel from the port city of Joppa thirty miles up the coast to Caesarea (named to honor Augustus Caesar!) to the home of a very Gentile and uncircumcised centurion in the Roman army (and Italian too!). Cornelius the centurion was a "God-fearer," a Gentile who believed in one God and had adopted the moral and ethical teaching of the Jews, but was still uncircumcised and considered outside the boundaries of Judaism proper. But Peter went obediently and cautiously, taking six circumcised believers with him. And the Scripture records, "While Peter was still speaking these words, the Holy Spirit came on all who heard the message. The circumcised believers who had come with Peter were astonished that the gift of the Holy Spirit had been poured out even on Gentiles" (Acts 10:44-45).

Connecting this pivotal event in the New Testament to the Old Testament is as subtle as it is astounding. The connecting point is Peter himself and where he was when the call came to him with the challenge to cross ethnic, religious and political boundaries that Peter had been taught not to cross since he was knee high to a Torah scroll. First, Jesus called Peter "Simon, son of Jonah" ("John" is a common translation) at key moments, like at his calling (John 1:42), at his declaration of Jesus' messiahship near Caesarea Philippi (Matthew 16:17) and at his recommissioning as a disciple to lead and provide for God's people (John 21:15-17). Peter's connection to Jonah may indicate a familial link to the Old Testament prophet, but for Jesus this connection certainly links Peter to Jonah's story. And Jonah's story contains two more astounding connections to Acts 10. Both episodes begin in Joppa and both concern the challenge of Jewish ministry to Gentiles.

Jonah's story begins with the word of the Lord coming to Jonah to "go to the great city of Nineveh" (Jonah 1:2). Nineveh was the capital of the Assyrian Empire, the empire that would conquer Samaria, the northern kingdom of Israel in 722–721 B.C., less than fifty years after Jonah's very reluctant visit. "Very reluctant" puts it mildly! The story continues, "But Jonah ran away from the LORD and headed for Tarshish. He went down to Joppa, where he found a ship bound for that port. After paying the fare, he went aboard and sailed for Tarshish to flee from the LORD" (Jonah 1:3).

However, Jonah learned through sea storms and being deep in the belly of a great fish that there is no place or time where one can flee the presence of the Lord (Psalm 139:7-8). But even when Jonah goes to Nineveh, he does so reluctantly, and even after the city repents of its pagan and idolatrous wickedness, the prophet complains to the Lord, "That is what I tried to forestall by fleeing to Tarshish. I knew that you are a gracious and compassionate God, slow to anger and abounding in love, a God who relents from sending calamity. Now, LORD, take away my life, for it is better for me to die than to live" (Jonah 4:2-3). Jonah did not want to call the Ninevites to repentance because he didn't like them. They weren't his people; they were awful people, dirty people and completely undeserving of God's love and grace. Jonah wanted nothing to do with them.

Jonah may have failed overall as a missionary with a heart of grace (the story ends with a deafening silence concerning the judgment of Jonah), but nearly eight centuries later God's steadfast love sticks with the plan, and this time Simon Peter, the son of Jonah, doesn't board a ship to run away from God's will but walks up the coast to Caesar's city itself to share the grace of God with people he had nothing in common with. And this became the birthplace of *koinonia*, a Greek word only found in Acts meaning to hold all things in common, an intimate sharing, interconnectedness, unity. Koinonia, the very heartbeat of the church.

◯ The Ancient Story and Our Story

Paul's summary admonition, first to the Ephesians and now to us, is to "submit to one another out of reverence for Christ" (Ephesians 5:21). Why? Because, as Paul writes, "Christ loved the church and gave himself up for her to make her holy, cleansing her by the washing with water through the word, and to present her to himself as a radiant church, without stain or wrinkle or any other blemish, but holy and blameless" (Ephesians 5:25-27). In the context of the need for mutual submission in marital, familial and household relationships (Ephesians 5:21–6:9), Paul affirms for the bride of Christ what Jesus affirms about the covenant relationship of marriage: "what God has joined together, let no one separate" (Matthew 19:6).

Paul's letter is reminding the bride of Christ of her "wedding vows" and wants the church to realize the importance of learning well how to "love one another" no matter what. Indeed, in better times, through worse times, whether abounding in riches or experiencing the poverty of sin, when functioning poorly in sickness or in times of healthy community, we learn what it means to love and cherish the church. This family even death will not part!

Psalm 133 begins, "How good and pleasant it is / when God's people live together in unity!" How good it all can be when we, like Peter, step out of our comfort zones to know and love people we have little in common with except the only thing that really matters, our union in Christ who is our peace. This koinonia is our witness to the world.

LOOKING AHEAD

Learning to love each other in the church leads the church to love the lost. The lost, like the pagans in Nineveh open to repentance or the Italian God-fearer willing to go only so far, are still not the limits of God's ministry of reconciliation. While we were his enemies Christ died for us. The grace of God has no boundaries and neither does the ministry of reconciliation.

Going Deeper

Judaism Before Jesus: The Events and Ideas That Shaped the New Testament World by Anthony J. Tomasino (InterVarsity Press, 2003) lends insight into Jewish-Gentiles relations and tensions that were hard for the church to overcome in the first century.

8 / The Mission of God Through the Church

LOOKING AHEAD

MEMORY VERSE: 2 Corinthians 5:19
BIBLE STUDY: 2 Corinthians 5:14–6:10
READING: Motivation for the Mission: The Love of Christ

The ministry of reconciliation begins with the reconciliation of the church in Christ, extends to the community relationships within the church and then becomes a manifestation of grace and ambassadorship of God's grace to the world.

 ## Bible Study Guide

After reading 2 Corinthians 5:14–6:10, spend some time reflecting on it with the following questions in mind before looking at the Reading.

1. What does Paul identify as the motivation for the proclamation and demonstration of the gospel and ministry in verses 14-15?

2. Both the gospel and the basic expectations for disciples are explained in verses 14-15. What is Paul's emphasis here compared with that in Romans 5:17-19 and 1 Corinthians 15:21-23?

3. "So" in verse 16 indicates the implications for believers due to God's love through the cross and the significant changes in Paul's life. In comparison, what is Paul's view of Jesus as Messiah before he believed, as reflected in Acts 7:57–8:1; 9:1-2?

4. Paul continues to consider this radical reorientation and reality of what it means to be "in Christ" in verses 17-19. Consider the following as you study these three verses:
   • Who initiates the transformation?

   • What is the relationship between one's conversion to Christ Jesus and the whole of life's reality?

5. What is the link between the "ministry of reconciliation" (v. 18) and the "message of reconciliation" (v. 19)?

6. In the original language of the New Testament, the word for "ambassadors" is in verb form, not a noun, and carries the idea of *being representatives*—in doing something. What is the relationship between engaging in the ministry and message of reconciliation and *being ambassadors* of Christ (v. 20)?

How is Paul himself being an ambassador to his readers in Corinth in verse 20? (Note the imperative command of Paul's final appeal.)

7. What is the connection between Paul's conclusion in verse 21 with his foundational beginning point in verses 14-15?

What is the outcome of this radical transformation to being "new" in Christ?

8. Connect the idea of "co-workers" in 2 Corinthians 6:1 with God's appeal in 2 Corinthians 5:20. Connect the idea of "righteousness" in 2 Corinthians 5:21 to Paul's urgency for the Corinthian Christians in 2 Corinthians 6:1. In 2 Corinthians 6:2, Paul quotes the prophet Isaiah (Isaiah 49:8; see also Isaiah 55:6 and Psalm 69:13). How does Paul conclude this thought for the Corinthians (2 Corinthians 6:2) regarding the work and person of Christ?

9. How does Paul reflect on his work as an ambassador in both a positive and negative sense in 2 Corinthians 6:3-4?

Connect this idea to the honest portrayal of Paul's life as an ambassador that he lists in verses 4-10. Note how Paul's "great endurance" (v. 4) is followed by three sets of three things that indicate this. How is each set of three (vv. 4, 5a and 5b are delineated by semicolons) distinct in its focus?

10. Verses 6-7 consist of two clear sets of four things that summarize the manifestation of the Holy Spirit in an ambassador's life. What is the character and activity of the ambassador in this section?

11. What does Paul list as *both* positive and negative outcomes in verses 8-10 (see a similar list in 2 Corinthians 4:8-9)? How does this connect with Paul's honest exposure of his life to his motivation for ministry in 2 Corinthians 5:14?

Reading: Motivation for the Mission: The Love of Christ

First-century Corinth was a wealthy, ambitious and status-conscious boom-town situated on a four-and-a-half-mile-long isthmus, a trade route linking the Greek mainland with the Peloponnese and the convenient shortcut for people and goods moving east and west in the northern Mediterranean. Rome conquered the Greek city-state in 146 B.C., but approximately one hundred years later, during the reign of Julius Caesar, the city was repopulated by ambitious and competitive freedmen from Rome (whose status was just above that of a slave in the empire) and began its development as a Roman colony. Thus, the wealth of Corinth was "new money," and the *nouveau riches* of the city exploited their status with a competitive and highly ambitious spirit that narrowed their vision to that concerning their own position and prosperity. Like any urban city today, there was a wide disparity between the wealthy and the poor. Most Corinthian Christians were not wealthy (1 Corinthians 1:26) and many were slaves (1 Corinthians 7:20-24), but it seems even that those of lower socioeconomic status in the church itself wanted to compete for a place of higher prestige and position.

The apostle Paul founded the church in Corinth during his second missionary journey (Acts 18:1-18), and during his eighteen months in the city he found that many of the competitive and class-conscious attitudes of the city accompanied the new believers into the church. Corinthian Christians still valued earthly power and human wisdom over the servanthood and humility demanded by the gospel (1 Corinthians 1:18–2:5). Corinthian Christians would compete over anything from who baptized them (1 Corinthians 1:10-17) to who had the best spiritual gifts (1 Corinthians 12:1–14:33)! Corinth was also long known for its tolerance of all sorts of sexual practices. Prostitution was viewed as part of the city's commerce, and more than a few of its many sacred sites and sanctuaries used temple slaves for all sorts of sexual activity as a part of worship or entertainment. Corinth was a challenging city in which to plant a healthy church!

Paul's first letter to the Corinthian Christians was not well received; many in the church resisted Paul's apostolic authority and his declaration of the gospel that focused on unity in Christ, no matter one's status in the world. Paul's first letter stepped on a lot of toes—from those who thought it was fine to let the poor in their congregations wait to partake of the Lord's Supper until the wealthy had dined and enjoyed the sacred feast (1 Corinthians 11:17-34), to the tolerance of incest and adultery (chaps. 5–7) and issues concerning idolatry (chaps. 8, 10). Second Corinthians in the New Testament may, in fact, be Paul's third letter to the Corinthian church, written after a very harsh letter and a short, painful visit (2 Corinthians 2:3).

Paul's overriding concern in second Corinthians is the need for the status-conscious Corinthian Christians to quit trying to model the church and its mission after their city and its marketing. Paul insists that the church needs to look like and be like (and even smell like!) Jesus in the world and to realize that not everyone will like that—some will find the "aroma of Christ" to be the fragrance of life, others like the stench of death. The Word of God must not be peddled for profit or to please people, because how the church smells to God is all that really matters (2 Corinthians 2:14-17). Paul urges the Christians of Corinth to renounce secret and shameful ways, to not use deception or distort the Word of God, but to share the Word of God clearly and to do so more conscious of what God thinks of the ministry than the response of others (2 Corinthians 4:1-2). This concern sets the context for the study passage of this chapter.

Paul begins in 2 Corinthians 5:14 by confessing that the love of Christ motivates the witness of the church in the world, not the world's response to the witness itself. Paul ends his argument in the text by making clear that the work and witness of the church in the world also won't seem blessed or successful if judged by our own experience. The disciple, like Paul, may undergo sleepless nights, beatings, hardships and hunger, or glory, good reports, joy and abundant blessing (2 Corinthians 6:4-10). The middle section of the passage deals with how the church is to see the very people to whom they declare the gospel. The church must see the world through the eyes of Christ (2 Corinthians 5:16-19). The church's ministry of God's reconciliation of the world has actually been accomplished in Christ (v. 19) and is borne on his shoulders, and the message of reconciliation is actually God's appeal and may not be changed to please the whims or preferences of others, or to protect or promote the status of the messenger. Christians are ambassadors (v. 20), representatives submissive and obedient to the ministry and message of the One who is their Head, the Lord Jesus Christ.

Paul reminds his first readers that the time for this ministry and message has been long awaited, "now is the time of God's favor, now is the day of salvation" (2 Corinthians 6:2). The Father's mission through the church (John 20:21), accomplished in Christ and empowered by the Spirit (Acts 1:8), is the commitment of the church, "so that in him we might become the righteousness of God" (2 Corinthians 5:21). When the church lives out the reality of its life in Christ, it manifests what it looks like to be made right with God in its ministry and mission. Being right with God looks like reconciliation, being at home with others in the body of Christ—no matter their social status, ethnic identity or spiritual gifts. And being right with God looks like reconciliation, the invitation for all to find their home in the church because there is no sinner beyond the reach of God's love, judgment and grace extended through the sacrifice of God's only Son (2 Corinthians 5:14-16, 19). It is this love, Christ's sacrifice, which motivates the church for this ministry of reconciliation.

Reading Study Guide

1. Make a list (long or short) of the responsibilities you may have as a part of your local congregation. What is your primary motivation (e.g., giftedness, need, enjoyment, fellowship with others)?

2. Have you ever felt discouraged or ineffective in something you have done as part of a church community? Why or why not?

    What have you learned through persistence?

    If you have ever quit something, what made this a wise decision or not?

3. How might the example of Christ's love help shape your attitude for service, as well as help sustain your motivation for service during difficulties? Take time to compare Paul's emphasis on the person and work of Christ to other expressions of this idea in the New Testament: Hebrews 4:15; 1 John 3:5; 1 Peter 2:22, which is a quote of Isaiah 53:9.

4. One work of the Spirit in our lives is helping us to see others as God sees them in Christ. Consider a person for whom this comes naturally. Think about a person who makes this difficult. Write a summary of 2 Corinthians 5:17. What does this mean in the light of each of these people (or people groups)?

What might this pivotal verse mean for the ministry and message, the work and witness, of your congregation as a whole?

5. Think about an experience of reconciliation between you and another that you may have experienced in your life. What was necessary for this to happen?

What did it cost you or the other person?

Consider how this reconciliation was or was not nurtured to grow into a good relationship.

6. Identify situations or issues where the church's ministry and message is needed in places like Corinth today. How does the church's identity as Christ's ambassadors help the church's faithfulness as the "aroma of Christ" in the world?

Identify situations or issues today where the church is tempted to be people pleasers or "peddlers of the gospel" (2 Corinthians 2:17).

7. Today is still the "time of God's favor" and the "day of salvation," and continues until the return of Christ Jesus. Identify a handful of people you know for whom you can be Christ's ambassador, carrying the message of reconciliation of God in Christ by the Spirit. Begin to pray daily for these people and follow God's lead into their lives where he is already at work preparing them for the message of reconciliation.

8. Consider potential "stumbling blocks" that can discredit your ministry or your congregation's ministry as an ambassador (2 Corinthians 6:3). How does endurance, especially in challenging places or with difficult people, help to commend you as Christ's servant (2 Corinthians 6:4)?

9. Take time to pray for yourself and the church in the world in the light of Paul's experience and steadfastness listed in 2 Corinthians 6:4-10. What is one thing you can do now to be a global-minded Christian in the world that God loves?

Connecting to the Old Testament

Jesus made it very clear that his messianic role was to fulfill, to bring to fullest reality, all that God—through Israel's law, history and prophetic witness—desired (Matthew 5:17-19). To fulfill does not mean to abolish or replace, but to bring to fullest expression so that nothing else is needed. Paul's declaration that "All this is from God, who reconciled us to himself though Christ" sums up how God condescended to make right all that had gone so wrong in the world from the very first moment of human rebellion. God's redemptive and reconciling work begins by building anticipation through the story of God's people recorded in the Hebrew Scripture and comes to its fullest expression through the incarnation of God in Jesus Christ, his death for all so that all who put their faith in him might live (Romans 3:22; Galatians 2:16; 3:26; 5:6; 2 Corinthians 5:14-15). This grand story is, in fact, one story of how the one true God reconciled the world to himself in Christ. Creation, as the intended arena of God's revelation of himself, became, after the Fall, the arena of salvation.

The message of reconciliation is given to the church as a community of heralds to proclaim to the world. The ministry of reconciliation is the demonstration by the church of what has been accomplished in Christ. As ambassadors, we carry a message that the war against sin, death and the devil is finished in Christ Jesus (John 16:7-11). The ministry and message committed to the church and empowered by the Spirit is not ours to change or tweak to fit the spirit of any age or the changing appetites of sin or even the most attractive of religious trends. The gospel of God is not a like a choose-your-own-adventure children's book where the reader decides the ending. The good news of Christ is fully told, and we can even read the last chapter and find out how it ends!

The story of God's reconciling work comes to its climax in Christ Jesus, but the plot and major characters are all there in the first three chapters of the Old Testament, and the drama unfolds with clarity and complexity, faithfulness and rebellion, lessons learned and forgotten, heroes and villains throughout the Old Testament. This story and these people belong to the church because only in the shadows of this story does the shape of salvation's full light come to be understood. This bright noonday is the story of the New Testament, the message of reconciliation entrusted to the community of the reconciled.

The New Testament letter to the Hebrews connects the anticipation and fulfillment of this story like this:

In the past God spoke to our ancestors thorough the prophets at many times and in various ways, but in these last days he has spoken to us by his Son, whom he appointed heir of all things, and through whom also he made the universe. The Son is the radiance of God's glory and the exact representation of his being, sustaining all things by his powerful word. After he had provided purification for sins, he sat down at the right hand of the Majesty in heaven. (Hebrews 1:1-3)

If you want a life of adventure, "Be reconciled to God. . . . [B]ecome the righteousness of God" (2 Corinthians 5:20-21). If you want a story worth telling, be a messenger of the good news of reconciliation in Christ Jesus. If you want a life that matters, be an ambassador of Christ and participate in God's adventure! Like Paul, you may not know what happens next (2 Corinthians 6:4-10), but you sure won't get bored along the way.

💬 The Ancient Story and Our Story

The ancient story is God's story. The gospel becomes our story through the reconciling work of Christ Jesus. However, even when we participate in God's story, it is not ours to change or modify along the way. It's tempting to modify the good news by leaving out the bad news that makes it necessary. At times, we're a whole lot like the Corinthians who wanted the aroma of Christ to smell sweeter in their city. In order to connect to the culture, like the Corinthians of old, some congregations find it pretty compelling to remove the cross from the sanctuary, suffering from the sermon or the confession of sin from a worship service. It's pretty easy to add promises of personally satisfying success to the gospel. The gospel doesn't promise an athlete a highlight-reel career or a scholar a better GPA. The gospel doesn't promise a perfect marriage partner or a guarantee of fertility needed for having children. Like the Corinthians, we want to fit in, we want the world to appreciate us, like us, accept us and empower us.

We want the gospel to find its place in the world instead of challenging the world to find its true home in the gospel. The Scripture makes it very clear that God "reconciled [the church] to himself through Christ" (2 Corinthians 5:18) and "was reconciling the world to himself in Christ" (v. 19)—and God's reconciliation moves but one way. Often Christians think about how to fit Christian faith and witness, the ministry and message of reconciliation, *into* our lives, but this is the "wrong direction." The biblical challenge from beginning to end is how our lives— who we are and what we do—fits *into* the gospel, the very life of Christ Jesus. The gospel is not an add-on to our lives, it is our life. And in the eyes of the world the gospel, the ministry and message of reconciliation, looks like weakness and foolishness. It looks like the cross. And when the world smells the aroma of Christ from the church in its midst, to some it smells like life itself and others turn their noses up in disgust because it smells like someone died.

Messengers of reconciliation need endurance, a willingness to suffer in order to be faithful to the message and its Author. We don't get to change the message to suit the audience. And we don't get to define what is successful concerning our faithfulness either. Jonah walked across Nineveh in a three-day ministry with a bad attitude and no love for the lost, and the city had a short-lived revival that made the evening news. Today, Jonah's results would merit him a TV show and a lifestyle that smelled like success. On the other hand, Isaiah had a lifelong ministry that people ignored, tuned out, shut off and didn't get. Isaiah ended up with a congregation of only about 10 percent of what he started with (Isaiah 6:9-13). Today, Isaiah's ministry would be subject to every suggestion and gimmick for a quick fix that would put him on the road to the kind of success that can be quantified and measured and then advertised. But with whom was God pleased? It's Isaiah, not Jonah, who sings the song of the Suffering Servant. And this is still the song of the church that smells like Jesus.

Looking Ahead

To sing the song of the Crucified in a culture that believes it deserves better, one must have the mind of Christ. To think like Jesus, to smell like Jesus, to live like Jesus means to live the self-emptying life in order to be full of Jesus, the one and only Son, who came from the Father, full of grace and truth. In his death we die; in his life we live; in his body we learn to love.

Going Deeper

It is important to understand the historical and cultural contexts of biblical texts. Every book of the New Testament was first written to a particular set of people in a specific context, and the more we understand God's first intention for his Word, the better we can understand it and apply it concretely to our lives. For instance, it's hard to more fully appreciate Paul's letters to the Corinthian Christians and the importance of his challenge to them without understanding Corinth, its history, cultures and people. *The Baker Illustrated Bible Handbook*, edited by Dan Hays and Scott Duvall (2011), is an exceptionally helpful volume to gain a good foundation for keeping the story of Scripture connected contextually.

The Story of Scripture, by Robbie Castleman, is an InterVarsity Press LifeGuide Bible Study (2011) that takes the student from Genesis to Revelation in twelve studies. It is helpful for those wanting an overview of the overarching story that the Old and New Testaments reveal. Having a good grasp of the metanarrative can help you locate and understand particular texts in the light of the whole.

Part Three

THE PRESENT AND COMING KINGDOM OF GOD

9 / Community Relationships

LOOKING AHEAD

MEMORY VERSES: Philippians 2:2-4
BIBLE STUDY: Philippians 1:29–2:16
READING: Having the Mind of Christ, Living in the Community of Faith

Having the mind of Christ Jesus is a call to a life that gives itself away for the sake of others. Losing one's life to find it—dying to self—is central, not just to salvation, but it is the continuing cost of discipleship for those who would follow Jesus.

 ## Bible Study Guide

After reading Philippians 1:29–2:16, spend some time reflecting on it with the following questions in mind before looking at the Reading.

1. Every "you" in this passage is a second-person plural, indicating the Philippian Christian community as a whole. In fact it is very rare for Paul's letters to use the singular "you." When he does it is used as a direct address to a particular person, like Timothy or Titus. The immediate context for Philippians 1:29 is the comment "you will be saved—and that by God" (Philippians 1:28). With this idea of divine grace in mind, what does Paul say this salvation entails for believers as well as for him in verses 29-30?

2. Note how "therefore" connects Philippians 2:1 with the ending of the first chapter of Philippians. In this connection, list the four "if" statements that Paul makes in verse 1. How are the persons of the Trinity involved in the dynamics of these statements?

3. Paul's "if" statements are directly connected to the first word in verse 2, *then*, the idea being "*if* this is true, *then* this must be as well." What is Paul's first "then" conclusion in verse 2?

4. Verse 2 continues with a list of what the Philippians need to embody for Paul's desired outcome to become a reality. Again, noting the trinitarian dynamics, how might you connect the three ideas Paul begins with in verse 2 with the "if" statements in the preceding verse?

5. Paul continues using the if-then structure of the text in a series of both positive and negative commands in verses 3-4. With what particular admonition does Paul end the list of these commands (v. 5)?

6. Paul then continues this idea in Philippians 2:6-8 by describing what the "mind of Christ" (or "mindset") looked like in Jesus as the incarnation of God. How would you summarize this profound statement in your own words?

7. Note the connection between verses 8 and 9, indicated by Paul's use of the word *therefore* and its similarity to the "therefore" in Philippians 2:1 as a connection to the end of chapter 1. What is the outcome of the Lord's incarnation, humiliation, self-emptying and obedience in verses 9-11?

What does the "therefore" in verse 9 communicate about the connection between humility and exaltation, both for Christ Jesus and, by implication, the Philippian community of faith?

8. Philippians 2:6-11, in conjunction with Paul's admonition and instruction in the first four verses of chapter 2, very likely indicates that Paul is aware of a problem in the Philippian community of faith. What do you think the problem may be that Paul begins to address in this section of the letter?

What are the connections between the language and wording of verses 1-4 and that of verses 6-8?

9. Philippians 2:12 begins with a third "therefore" in this passage. After Paul addresses the Philippian believers (v. 12), he concludes his challenge to them. What is the command Paul gives for the church to obey as the focus of the "therefore" in verse 12?

What help does Paul immediately connect to this command to encourage the obedience of the faith community (v. 13)?

10. Verse 14 may indicate part of the problem in the Philippian community of faith. In verses 15-16 Paul quickly follows the negative aspect of his command in verse 14 by highlighting the outcome of having the mind of Christ through a lifetime of similar self-emptying obedience. If you were a part of the Philippian community Paul first wrote to, what might you feel or think or want to do when you first heard these promises?

👓 Reading: Having the Mind of Christ, Living in the Community of Faith

Philippi was located on the Egnatian Way, a major east-west trade route, and Macedonia was an area northeast of the Greek peninsula bordering the Aegean Sea. Paul, along with Silas and Luke, founded the church in Philippi (A.D. 49) during his second missionary journey in response to the vision of a man of Macedonia pleading for help (Acts 16:9-10). This vision may have been necessary because Philippi is unlike many of the cities where Paul initiated his missionary work. Paul routinely began his work with Jews, meeting in a synagogue in each city, but Philippi's Jewish population was so small that it lacked the ten married men required to have a synagogue. However, in obedience to the vision, Paul and his companions still went down to the river in Philippi on the sabbath to find the small Jewish community (Acts 16:13). The apostle knew faithful Jews would meet near the river for the ritual of hand washing in running water in preparation for prayer.

Although Paul's vision was that of a Macedonian man, the record of Paul's mission in Philippi begins and ends with a woman named Lydia (Acts 16:12-15; 16:40). Acts 16:14-15 describes Lydia as a "dealer in purple cloth" from Thyatira, a city in the Roman province, who was a "worshiper of God," whose house and household are identified in Acts as belonging to her. Lydia, much like Cornelius the centurion in Acts 10:2, was probably a Gentile God-fearer, a person faithful to the one God of Judaism and a keeper of the Jewish moral law. Philippians is the only letter of Paul without a direct quote of the Old Testament, and this may be because many Gentiles were unfamiliar with the Hebrew Scripture.

Philippi was an ancient city, named after the father of Alexander the Great, and after rebuilding the city on its own after the conquest of the Romans, Philippi earned the elite status as a Roman colony. The situation in Philippi at the time of Paul's writing adds historical and political texture to the letter as a part of Paul's appeal to the church and its life and witness in a very challenging city. Paul uses Philippian pride in their status as citizens of a Roman colony to remind the church of their true citizenship (Philippians 3:20). Paul mentions his effective witness to "the palace guard" (Philippians 1:13). These Praetorian guards were select troops of the emperor who Paul had contact with during his imprisonment near Rome.[1]

Philippians 2:6-11 has long been considered by many to be one of the first summary statements of the faith (like an early creed) in the early church. It may be a major statement that Paul used in his teaching as he planted congregations throughout the empire. If so, this rather poetic statement may have been very familiar to the Philippian believers, possibly something that they sang as an early hymn or recited like a creed. Philippi had a population that was fiercely loyal to the empire and the Roman emperor Nero, whose most prominent titles used at the time of Paul's letter (c. A.D. 62) were "lord" and "savior." The supremacy of the risen and ascended Savior and Lord in Philippians 2:9-11 is a direct challenge to honoring Nero with these titles at every public event in the colony. No wonder that just a few years after Paul wrote this letter, Nero began his persecution against Christians in the empire!

Paul's imprisonment and the dynamics of Paul's relationship to the Philippian believers are significant to the overall content of the letter. Unlike the church in Corinth, the Christians in Philippi were fiercely loyal to Paul as their founding apostle, so much so Paul had to remind them that the gospel of the Lord Jesus was central, not any missionary, pastor or teacher (Philippians 1:15-18). Part of the Philippian letter is a "thank you note" for a gift from the Christian community brought to Paul by Epaphroditus, a leader in the church (Philippians 2:25-30; 4:10-18). Paul also warns the church to be aware of zealous Jews within certain Christian communities who came to Philippi claiming that only through fully identifying with rituals of Judaism, like circumcision, could one belong to the family of the Messiah. Paul calls these people who pervert the gospel of grace with genealogical pride "dogs," "evildoers" and "mutilators of the flesh" (Philippians 3:2). The entire third chapter of Philippians deals with this

likely threat to the predominantly Gentile church in Philippi.

However, throughout the letter there are hints that there is significant conflict brewing in this beloved community of faith. Something is disrupting the unity of the church that is not rooted in some heretical doctrine that the church has embraced (or Paul would have addressed this directly!), but in a dispute between two leaders in the community over something that Paul leaves unidentified in the letter. Paul's intentional omission of the specific issue behind the dispute makes two things clear. First, the issue itself is not the problem and, therefore, is of no interest to Paul. And, second, the real problem is the conflict between the two leaders, women named Euodia and Syntyche, which threatens to split the church in Philippi. Not until Paul nears the end of the letter does the apostle finally "name names" and directly apply the major theme of the letter to these specific women (Philippians 4:2-9). Paul's need to carefully and clearly address these two leaders concerning the damage their dispute is causing to the Philippian church is the cohesive element that connects every part of the letter. These two leaders, and by extension the whole church, need to think long and hard about Jesus, the Head of the church, and learn to follow his example in their relationships with one another.

Having the "mind of Christ" means a life full of "tenderness and compassion," a life of "humility" that values "others above yourselves" and looks to "the interest of the others" (Philippians 2:1-4). This is what Paul exhorts Euodia and Syntyche to embrace (Philippians 4:2). Paul calls these two women "co-workers" with whom he "contended" for the "cause of the gospel" (Philippians 4:3). In fact, Euodia and Syntyche may have been among the women Paul first met in Philippi (Acts 16:13), those Paul prays for with joy because of their "partnership in the gospel from the first day until now" (Philippians 1:5). Along with the whole church, Paul challenges these women to embrace the self-emptying life of the Savior, who did not use even his "equality with God" as something to exploit for "his own advantage" (Philippians 2:6). Euodia and Syntyche may have been equals in the mission of the church, but they were exploiting their position and gifts "out of selfish ambition or vain conceit" (Philippians 2:3).[2]

Paul wants Euodia and Syntyche, along with the entire church in Philippi, to understand that having the mind of Christ means sharing the self-emptying life of humility, servanthood and obedience of Jesus. Like the Savior, only the cross-bearing life of dying to self ends in glory. The expression translated "vain conceit" in Philippians 2:3 is literally the word meaning "empty glory" in Greek. Paul uses this play on words to make the point that only

in the self-emptying life is true glory to be found. This is the exaltation of the Servant Son by God the Father that Paul celebrates in Philippians 2:9-11. "Jesus Christ is Lord" (Philippians 2:11), not Caesar, and certainly not Euodia or Syntyche. Having the mind of Christ means "not looking to your own interests" (Philippians 2:4), and in the light of the exalted Savior, it means that Euodia and Syntyche need to "Rejoice in the Lord always," letting their "gentleness be evident to all"; they should "not be anxious about anything" but pray together (Philippians 4:4-6). Paul reminds these women, and the disgruntled community, that God is at work in them and works to help them mature (Philippians 1:6) and that "the Lord is near" (Philippians 4:5), and it is his "peace . . . which transcends all understanding" (Philippians 4:7). Finally, Euodia and Syntyche need to sit down with each other, like every member of the church in Philippi, and "think about" and learn to rejoice in whatever is true, noble, right, pure, lovely, admirable, excellent or praiseworthy in each other (Philippians 4:8).

Having the mind of Christ takes practice (Philippians 4:9) and it takes a lifetime to learn (Philippians 1:6). But "with fear and trembling," those who declare that Jesus is Lord learn to "work out" the salvation that God "works in" us (Philippians 2:12-13).

---

[1]See Philippians 4:22 for another indication of Paul's ministry to the most "unlikely" people.

[2]I've often wondered whether these two women heard this part of Paul's letter when it was first read to the gathered congregation in Philippi and thought to themselves, "Oh, I hope she's listening!"

Reading Study Guide

1. Think about the if-then structure Paul uses in the early verses of Philippians 2, and consider situations in your own life when you have either used or been subject to this sort of teaching dynamic. For instance, it is not uncommon for parents to use a similar language structure to help their children anticipate positive or negative consequences for making certain choices: "If you don't brush your teeth, then . . . ," "If you study hard, then . . . ," and so forth. Consider Paul's specific if-then content in Philippians 2:1-4 and summarize your own history of being challenged with this teaching.

2. Take some time to meditate on the life and death of the Lord Jesus as Paul reflects on his suffering in the incarnation in Philippians 2:6-8. When have you found the self-emptying life difficult and obedience to God costly?

3. Consider Paul's summary exaltation in Philippians 2:9-11 with his teaching in Romans 10:9-13. What does it mean to confess "Jesus is Lord" in your life and faith community? How would you explain this to a ten-year-old, a teenager, your best friend and someone who might challenge your confession?

4. Make a list of specific ways you experience God at work in your life (Philippians 1:6; 2:12-13). What are some concrete ways you can "work out" your salvation or make more manifest your sanctification in your journey of faith?

5. Less than 10 percent of the Roman Empire was literate in the first century, so all the writings of that time were meant to be read out loud. Read aloud the entire letter to the Philippians while pretending to be one of the congregational leaders, either Euodia or Syntyche. Honestly consider what Euodia or Syntyche might have felt or thought as they heard the letter read to the congregation. For example, see footnote 2 of this study. How do you think nondoctrinal disputes can de-energize and distract the church from its witness and work?

6. Make plans with someone in your congregation to meet, discuss and pray together about the dynamics of self-emptying love both within your faith community and its relationship with local and global ministry and mission.

Connecting to the Old Testament

The prophet Hosea lived in the eighth century B.C. during the decline of the northern kingdom of Israel and its eventual conquest by the Assyrians in 722. The Old Testament book that bears his name focuses on how Hosea's life and prophetic voice reflected the steadfast love for God's unfaithful and wayward people as well as the reality of divine discipline and judgment they needed. The first three chapters of the book narrate the hopes and heartbreak of Hosea's marriage to a woman named Gomer, who was unfaithful throughout their betrothal and marriage. Through the turbulence of their relationship, Gomer had three children. Hosea 1:3-4 makes it clear that Hosea fathered the first child, a son God directed to be named Jezreel, meaning "God scatters," as a prophetic living sermon pointing to the impending doom of Israel. The text is ambiguous about the paternity of Gomer's next two children, a daughter, again at divine direction named Lo-Ruhamah, meaning "not loved," and a son named Lo-Ammi, meaning "not my people." Throughout the narrative, God directs Hosea to love his wife, to rescue her from bad situations, to speak the truth in love to her, to bring her home again and again. The story of Hosea's obedience to God in loving Gomer is a story of self-emptying love. The prophetic passages in the Old Testament book reveal the self-emptying love of God for his people.

The story of Hosea illustrates the teaching of Hebrews 12:1-12. The writer of the letter to the Hebrews, like the apostle Paul in Philippians, lifts up Jesus as the supreme example of the obedience and self-giving necessary to live and to love, and to persevere in both as people who belong to God. As beloved children who struggle with the self-emptying life, we are to fix

> our eyes on Jesus, the pioneer and perfecter of faith. For the joy set before him he endured the cross, scorning its shame, and sat down at the right hand of the throne of God. Consider him who endured such opposition from sinners, so that you will not grow weary and lose heart. (Hebrews 12:2-3)

The text in Hebrews goes on to say, using passages from Psalms and Proverbs, that the Lord "disciplines the one he loves. . . . Endure hardship as discipline; God is treating you as his children. . . . If you are not disciplined . . . then you are not legitimate, not true sons and daughters at all" (Hebrews 12:6-8).

Paul concludes Philippians 1:29–2:16 with a series of promises in verses 14-16. In this section Paul subtly extends the promises given to God's people in the Old Testament to his young brothers and sisters in Philippi. With an echo of Israel's "grumbling and arguing" (v. 14) in the wilderness journey out of Egypt (Exodus 16:12), Paul ends up using the language of Deuteronomy 32:5. Unlike the Israelites who were "corrupt and not his children; . . . a warped and crooked generation," the Philippians are to be "blameless and pure, 'children of God without fault in a warped and crooked generation'" (v. 15). Finally, Paul uses Daniel's language, the wise "will shine like the brightness of the heavens, and those who lead many to righteousness, like the stars for ever and ever" (Daniel 12:3), as the ultimate hope for the church to "shine among them like stars in the sky as you hold firmly to the word of life" (vv. 15-16).

◯ The Ancient Story and Our Story

Although the sin of Euodia and Syntyche certainly fell short of the idolatry of Israel, Paul was willing to embody the discipline of God's love for and claim on their lives. Paul was willing to live the self-emptying life he saw in Jesus (he explicitly acknowledges this in Philippians 2:17) and was willing to be God's hand of loving discipline in calling his partners in the gospel to join him on this hard road to glory. Paul reminds the Philippians that God had begun a good work in them and wasn't about to give up when the going got tough. The Lord did not abandon Israel. Hosea did not fail in his fidelity to Gomer. Paul died at the hand of the emperor. And the day will come when every knee will bow and every tongue will confess that Jesus, the obedient and crucified Christ, is Lord. And God continues to discipline those he loves while he brings the church to completion until that day.

It's also good to notice that although Paul's supreme example of the self-emptying life is the Lord Jesus, he offers himself (Philippians 2:17-18), Timothy (Philippians 2:19-23) and their own pastor, Epaphroditus (Philippians 2:25-30), as "mere" human examples of the self-emptying life of love and faithfulness. This is certainly a relief, not just to the Philippians but to us. It reminds me of the time a father in our congregation called us on a Sunday afternoon with a chuckle in his voice. He wanted to tell us what his five-year-old son said when asked if Jesus would have hit his three-year-old sister in the head, completely unprovoked, by the way. This father said his son looked at him and said (while his sister was crying her eyes out), "Well, no, but I don't walk on water either." Like this five-year-old, we need non-Son of God examples to help us live the Christian life step by step, day by day. We are all slow to learn how to love through a self-emptying life, but God is at work until we come out right and shine like stars forever.

Looking Ahead

It's clear, with rare exception, that the kingdom journey for the Christian is a marathon and not a sprint. "Training in righteousness" (2 Timothy 3:16) is what it takes to finish a spiritual triathlon. Training for the race includes mentoring by elders in the faith, knowing God's Word, recognizing one's calling, using spiritual gifts well and saying no to the junk food temptations of the world that quench the disciple's appetite for the nourishment of the training table. Study 10 will help us understand how the self-emptying life is also full and satisfying.

Going Deeper

Eugene Peterson's classic *A Long Obedience in the Same Direction* is an insightful devotional handbook on the life of faith (InterVarsity Press, 2000). Peterson uses the pilgrim songs of Israel as a framework to reflect on the realities and challenges of being faithful to God in a world that doesn't cheer you on. This is a book you will want to keep and read again and again.

10 / Community of Integrity and Character

LOOKING AHEAD

MEMORY VERSE: 2 Timothy 2:15
BIBLE STUDY: 2 Timothy 3:10–4:8
READING: Life as a Relay

The character of leaders in the church is more important than their job descriptions. Spirit-filled and Spirit-led leadership for God's people is as critical an issue for the church today as it was in the emerging church structures of the New Testament.

 Bible Study Guide

After reading 2 Timothy 3:10–4:8, spend some time reflecting on it with the following questions in mind before looking at the Reading.

1. Paul begins his address to Timothy ("you" in verse 10 is singular, indicating a direct address) by summarizing his relationship with the younger disciple in verses 10-11. Note the repetition of the word *my* in Paul's statement and list both the positive and negative aspects of Paul's life that Timothy has shared with the apostle. How would these experiences help deepen Timothy's knowledge of Paul and his ministry?

2. Noting how Paul takes the spotlight off himself in verse 12, how does this model a good thing for Timothy to understand, both for himself and his own ministry and his work with other believers?

How does Paul's contrasting comment in verse 13 underscore this point?

3. Note the repetition of the singular word *you* as Paul focuses on Timothy in particular and addresses him with an imperative reminder in verse 14. In light of this admonition to Timothy, what might the deceptive "evildoers and impostors" (v. 13) be doing from within the church itself?

4. Read 2 Timothy 1:5 to better understand Paul's comment about Timothy's lifelong knowledge of "Holy Scriptures" (2 Timothy 3:15). How does Paul describe the outcome of this immersion in Scripture for Timothy?

5. Paul uses a particular formula for an authoritative "charge" three times in 1 and 2 Timothy (see 1 Tim 5:21; 6:13-14; 2 Tim 4:1). Second Timothy 4:1 is the introduction to the third charge to the young pastor. Paul emphasizes three distinct ideas in this introduction that give sober weight, authority and perspective for the charge itself. What are these three and why are they important?

6. Identify the central charge Paul gives Timothy in the opening words of 2 Timothy 4:2. Summarize Paul's major points in verse 2 by answering the following questions:
   • What is necessary for faithfulness to the charge?

- What is this faithfulness intended to accomplish?

- How is the charge to be carried out?

7. Second Timothy 4:3-4 summarizes why Paul thought this charge to Timothy was important. What is Paul's assessment of what Timothy can expect during his time of ministry (and to the present day)?

8. Paul's focus returns to Timothy, again by the use of a singular "you" in verse 5, and he completes his charge to Timothy with four additional imperatives. Why are these important in Christian ministry?

9. Paul concludes this passage (vv. 6-8) with a reflection on his impending death and completes the "baton pass" of his life's relay to Timothy. How do Paul's words in this text compare with those of Philippians 2:17-18?

How does this conclusion (v. 8) compare with the introduction to Paul's charge to Timothy in verse 1?

👓 Reading: Life as a Relay

The background of Paul's relationship to Timothy is important in understanding this affectionate and challenging final word from Paul to his "dear son" (2 Timothy 1:2). In 2 Timothy 3:11 Paul mentions three towns in Asia Minor: Antioch (Pisidian), Iconium and Lystra. Locate these three cities on a map showing Paul's first missionary journey (with his mentor in the faith, Barnabas). Acts 13:42–14:22 provides a sense of the persecutions Paul is referring to. Timothy was raised by a Christian mother in Lystra, and he would have been well aware of Paul's ministry and his persecution in his hometown and nearby cities. During his second missionary journey Paul intentionally returned to Lystra, where the apostle called Timothy to join him in ministry (Acts 16:1-5).[1]

Paul's epistles to Timothy and Titus were written during the apostle's imprisonment during the heightened time of Nero's persecution in the early A.D. 60s. However, 1–2 Timothy and Titus are not known as Prison Epistles (like Philippians, Ephesians, Colossians and Philemon) but as Pastoral Epistles because these three letters are full of advice for Paul's younger partners in the pastoral, evangelistic and missionary work of the gospel. It seems that the Prison Epistles and the Pastoral Epistles were written during two very different circumstances. After Paul was seized by Jewish authorities in Jerusalem and rescued from certain death by a Roman

commander because Paul was a Roman citizen, two years passed waiting for formal charges to be filed against him. Acts 21:27–28:31 details the intriguing account of Paul's life during this time. The apostle's witness to the gospel spread from the mob in Jerusalem to his defense of the faith before the Sanhedrin council, to officials in Caesarea, to a regional king, Agrippa II, to pagan sailors during a shipwreck on the way to Rome, to a chief official Paul healed on the island of Malta, to Rome and the constant presence of Praetorian guards. Luke concludes the book of Acts with this summary comment: "For two whole years Paul stayed there in his own rented house and welcomed all who came to see him. He proclaimed the kingdom of God and taught about the Lord Jesus Christ—with all boldness and without hindrance!" (Acts 28:30-31). The four Prison Epistles were written during this time period (c. A.D. 60–62).

It seems that formal charges were never filed, and Paul's accusers never arrived from Jerusalem. Paul, protected by his right as a Roman citizen, would have been automatically released after a two-year house detention.[2] Acts makes it clear that Rome was very hesitant to settle matters they considered a Jewish religious dispute (see Acts 18:11-17; 19:23-41 for examples prior to Paul's seizure in Jerusalem). Other than the Pastoral Epistles, the New Testament does not include any details about

Paul's second arrest and imprisonment other than to make very clear that it was far more severe than the first-century Roman version of an "ankle bracelet" to keep the apostle housebound. Second Timothy, Paul's last letter, is sprinkled with comments that betray Paul's longing and loneliness (2 Timothy 1:4; 4:9-11, 21). And the text in this passage makes it very clear that his execution is certain (2 Timothy 4:6-7). Second Timothy functions much like the "Farewell Discourse" of Jesus in John's Gospel (John 13:31–18:2). Paul is preparing his disciple for the increasing responsibility of leadership in the church after his death.

Timothy is a well-matured Christian, but still quite young when Paul passes the baton of ministry to him and to Titus. Paul seems concerned that some in Ephesus may think Timothy's age may cause some to question or not respect his authority (1 Timothy 4:12). Timothy may have been an older teenager at the beginning of their partnership in Lystra (Acts 16:1-3). Timothy's experience may have been much like John's when Jesus called him and his brother James into discipleship. If fifteen years had passed since Timothy joined Paul during the second missionary journey, Timothy may have been in his late twenties or early thirties when Paul wrote his first letter to him asking for help in opposing the false teachers in Ephesus (1 Timothy 1:3-4). Paul trusted Timothy as a worthy partner in the gospel in difficult situations (1 Thessalonians 3; 1 Corinthians 4:16-17; 16:10-11; Philippians 2:19-24)

even though Timothy may have been timid or overwhelmed at times (1 Corinthians 16:10-11; 2 Timothy 1:6-8) and in need of advice for his own health (1 Timothy 5:23). With this in mind it is important to remember when reading the Pastoral Epistles that Paul's tone for his directives is entrusted to two disciples who he is confident will use what he says with the wisdom and love needed for ministry.

In Paul's two letters addressed to Timothy, the apostle includes three charges to the young pastor-missionary. The first charge includes a challenge to attend to the whole letter, a general admonition for ministry and advice for Timothy's moral life and physical well-being (1 Timothy 5:21-23). The second charge comes after Paul addresses Timothy as a "man of God" who is to avoid the love of money and any attempt to get rich through the ministry of the gospel (1 Timothy 6:6-10) and underscores the need for Timothy to "keep this command without spot or blame" (v. 14). This second charge is followed by one of Paul's most eloquent doxologies (vv. 15-16). The charge at the beginning of 2 Timothy 4 centers on the vital importance of preaching with a learned and well-focused fidelity to God's Word no matter the season, the temperament or preferences of the audience or the spirit of the age.

Paul knew Timothy's understanding of Holy Scripture was vitally important to his ministry. Like Paul, Timothy had a story to tell, not just propositional truths to argue. God breathed his story through real people with situational particularity—

in real time, in real places, with real concerns. From Sinai in the Old Testament to Caesarea in the New, what emerges as Holy Scripture is a story. Scripture isn't written as a list of dos and don'ts that disembodies the truth and renders biblical scholarship a practice of pathology on a dead thing that is cut up and put together to prove a point or make a diagnosis of some kind. The Pharisee Paul had been that kind of pathologist! Like Paul before his confrontation by the living, breathing Lord Jesus on the road to Damascus, the religio-political party faithfuls that Jesus encountered knew the law, but not the Lawgiver. They ripped the truth from the narrative, and in losing the story they did not recognize the Messiah of Scripture when he stood in front of them. Paul himself took about three years off by himself to study the God-breathed Word through the presence and discipline of God's Spirit in order to see what he had missed and to understand why he missed it (Galatians 1:11-24). Paul had come to understand that the goal of sound doctrine wasn't to win an argument but "love, which comes from a pure heart and a good conscience and a sincere faith" (1 Timothy 1:5). The God-breathed Scripture is meant to help us know God, not just know more about him. The Scripture is not a self-protective weapon to be used against others but the unique witness God breathed through his servants that is an invitation to participate in a story, the divine drama of God's love for the world.

Paul's understanding of this story had its uniquely authoritative limit of the Hebrew Scripture. However, the New Testament itself begins to elevate the apostolic witness to the gospel of Jesus Christ to its equal status with the Old Testament. With the recognition of the early church as its preeminent leader, Peter makes this startling comment concerning Paul's writings near the end of Peter's second epistle,

> Bear in mind that our Lord's patience means salvation, just as our dear brother Paul also wrote you with the wisdom that God gave him. He writes the same way in all his letters, speaking in them of these matters. His letters contain some things that are hard to understand, which ignorant and unstable people distort, *as they do the other Scriptures,* to their own destruction. (2 Peter 3:15-16, emphasis added)

This text is the beginning of the process that will yield the New Testament canon with its unique authoritative status for the church. The late F. F. Bruce summarized the importance of Holy Scripture for Paul, Timothy and Christians throughout the ages, stating, "The New Testament books did not become authoritative for the church because they were formally included in a canonical list [in the fourth-century councils]; on the contrary, the church included them in her canon because she already regarded them as divinely inspired [God-breathed]."[3]

Last, Paul's sense of impending death is the atmosphere for this last letter of Paul in the New Testament. Although he longs to see Timothy (2 Timothy 4:9), his son in the Lord (2 Timothy 1:2), again, he knows that death is the doorway through which he can rest from his labors. Secure in Christ (Philippians 1:21, 23), Paul can anticipate Christ's "appearing and his kingdom" (2 Timothy 4:1). The God who began a good work in Paul has brought him to completion (Philippians 1:6). With Peter, who also died under the manic wrath of Nero, Paul is confident in the ending (which is really the beginning!) of God's story, and with all the saints, "in accordance with his promise, we wait for a new heaven and a new earth, where righteousness is at home" (2 Peter 3:13 NRSV).

---

[1]Although Paul steadfastly denied the necessity for Gentiles to be circumcised in order to be fully identified with God's people as a basis for salvation, the apostle circumcised Timothy for the sake of the mission Paul called him to. Without this rite, Timothy could not have participated in his inaugural work among the Jews. Paul was willing to "become all things to all people" (1 Corinthians 9:22) for the sake of the gospel's mission, but only "Jesus Christ and him crucified" (1 Corinthians 2:2) was necessary for salvation itself. Since only Timothy's mother is mentioned in the New Testament, it is generally assumed that Timothy's father was a Gentile, and although his father allowed Timothy to be raised as a Christian, he would not allow his circumcision as an infant according to Jewish law.

[2]Clement of Rome, in the late first century, mentions that Paul journeyed to "the extreme limits of the west" (1 Clement 5:6-7). And two second-century documents, the Murtorian Canon and the *Acts of Paul*, indicate that Paul left Rome for Spain. Recalling that Jonah tried to avoid a ministry to Gentiles by taking a boat from Joppa with the intention of taking it all the way to Tarshish (Jonah 1:3) in southern Spain, it is fitting that Paul may have made this journey to take the good news of Christ Jesus to "the ends of the earth" (Acts 1:8).

[3]F. F. Bruce's classic *The New Testament Documents: Are They Reliable?* carefully and compellingly makes a well-focused case for how the New Testament documents themselves attest to the historical claims of the texts more than any other ancient texts. The Scripture of the New Testament is the apostolic eyewitness to the revelation of God in the incarnation of God in time and space in Jesus of Nazareth. Bruce maintains that the "historical 'once-for-all-ness' of Christianity . . . makes the reliability of the writings which purport to record this revelation a question of first-rate importance" (F. F. Bruce, *The New Testament Documents: Are They Reliable?* [Downers Grove, IL: Inter-Varsity Press, 1981], p. 2). This brief (only 124 pages) book is a must-read for all students of the New Testament!

Reading Study Guide

1. Think about who you know among friends or family that know "all about" (2 Timothy 3:10) your way of life, your life's purpose, why you believe what you believe and the ups and downs of your life's experiences. Consider how those who know you this well have been matured in the faith because of this knowledge. Is there someone you know or have known who has shared his or her life with you in the way Paul did for Timothy?

2. Think back on your introduction to and study of Scripture during your journey as a Christian. Who have been your influential teachers?

   How have you experienced correction, discipline and "training in righteousness" through the Scripture?

3. How does God's Word help equip you "for every good work" (2 Timothy 3:17), not just for special occasions or events but for normal daily life?

   What are good next steps for you to continue "training in righteousness" as you participate in the story of Scripture by knowing God through his Word?

4. Remember that the Old Testament was Timothy's sole experience and understanding of Paul's reference to Scripture in 2 Timothy 3:16-17. Read 2 Peter 1:20-21 and take time to think about how the story and teaching in the Old Testament has been "useful" in your life for "rebuking, correcting and training in righteousness" (2 Timothy 3:16) and helpful in equipping you "for every good work" (v. 17).

5. Consider Paul's list of imperatives for Timothy in 2 Timothy 4:5 and think about people in your life who have done these things well and helped mature your faith in Christ. Make a list of people who have faithfully taught you God's Word (Hebrews 13:7). If possible, write them thank you notes about the ongoing influence this has had in your life.

6. Take time to write your own farewell letter to those you love, and share with them what you want them to know about your life and what you learned about God's faithfulness, the cost of discipleship and your own sense of longing "for his appearing."

➲ Connecting to the Old Testament

The stories of Abraham and Sarah, Moses, David, Daniel, Haggai and Nehemiah are honest pictures of people learning how to be faithful to the God who had called them to a particular life full of the work he had prepared for them to do. The Scriptures do not "stainglass" the saints of old. David is known in the Scripture as a man after God's own heart in both Testaments (1 Samuel 13:14, quoted in Paul's sermon in Pisidian Antioch, which Timothy may have heard in Acts 13:22), but he sinned against the Lord with the wife of Uriah and had children who grieved him deeply. Peter, the acknowledged head of the early church, was rebuked publicly by Paul (Galatians 2:11-21) and learned a hard lesson about racism and hypocrisy. Honesty is part of mentoring others well in life, and

Scripture is the supreme mentor—it tells us a true story, full sound and fury, beauty and warts, the good, the bad, and the ugly. This is one reason the story Scripture tells rings true with people. Reading Scripture describes our own lives and we know it. The journey of faith is not a Disneyland ride of faux excitement taken without risk on the safety of rails.[1] Real life is often a shallow kiddie pool offering only tepid refreshment in the heat of the day, and sometimes life feels like an unexpected flash flood that threatens to sweep away all that you know and love.

One way the pilgrims of the Old Testament learned the truth about life and how to trust God with the journey was through the psalms of ascent. Psalms 120–134 are the songs sung by pilgrims on their way up to the house of the Lord in Jerusalem for various festivals. These fifteen psalms are carefully arranged in five groups of three distinct movements. The first psalm of each set is honest about life's challenges and problems that pilgrims face along the way. The second psalm in each set looks to the character of God, who has the power to guide and rescue, and often this is set in contrast to those whose gods are deceptive and without real power to save. The third set of each triplet celebrates some aspect of God's peace, the shalom of the only true security in life. The psalms of ascent provide a beautifully honest picture of real life in the world in which we are "foreigners and exiles" (1 Peter 2:11) on a journey to the new Jerusalem, the kingdom of God where we pilgrims of righteousness are finally at home.

The Ancient Story and Our Story

In all three Pastoral Epistles Paul emphasizes the importance of "sound doctrine." The Greek word for "sound" is related to the English word used for hygiene or hygienic. "Sound" doctrine and "sound" teaching lead to healthy Christians and healthy congregations (for example, 1 Timothy 1:10; 6:3; 2 Timothy 1:13; 4:3; Titus 1:9). And sound doctrine is grounded in the knowledge of God's Word, which is preached, taught and lived in the life of believers. Knowing the story of Scripture is vital if we are to know that the One in whom we put our faith is the God revealed in the Scripture and not a god fashioned out of our own needs or culturally encrusted imagination. All of us are prone to gather around a great number of teachers to say what we want our itching ears to hear (Paul's warning in 2 Timothy 4:3-4). The well-respected New Testament scholar F. F. Bruce rightly maintains that "the character of Jesus can be known only from New Testament records."[2]

The teaching of sound doctrine is never "off the cuff" but demands preparation (2 Timothy 4:2) and the capacity to stick to "what you have learned . . . and known [from] the Holy Scriptures" (2 Timothy 3:14-15). Even today those who teach and preach God's Word need to spend more time in the study of the Scripture itself than looking for clever or entertaining add-ons, jokes or illustrations. Like Timothy, it takes time for us to be prepared to feed others with the Word of life. And this takes a commitment to the study of God's Word. The majority of the time it takes to preach a sermon or teach a lesson should be focused on the text of Scripture itself. Scripture, Paul says, is what it takes to thoroughly equip people for "every good work" (2 Timothy 3:16-17).

Scripture is a story about who God is, who we are, what went wrong and what God has done, is doing, and will do to make it right. This story belongs to God's people and we must know it well so that we can sing its songs honestly and lovingly as pilgrims on life's journey.

LOOKING AHEAD

Paul faced his death with confidence in God's steadfast love and saving grace known by the gift of faith in Christ Jesus by the Spirit. Jesus, because he knew who he was and where he was going (John 13:1), poured water into a basin and washed the feet of his disciples. In the same way, because Paul knew who he was and where he was going, he poured his life into his disciples and knew his work was finished (2 Timothy 4:6-7). Paul told the Philippians that all he wanted was to know Christ, and having participated in the suffering of the Savior, to know the power of the resurrection and to become like him in his death (Philippians 3:10-11). The reality of the resurrection is the focus of study 11, which is essential for understanding the New Testament.

Going Deeper

F. F. Bruce's *The New Testament Documents: Are They Reliable?* is a wonderful book that helps address all sorts of issues concerning how the New Testament canon was shaped. This is a valuable text for being prepared "in season and out of season" to responsibly bear witness to others concerning the texts of the New Testament.

---

[1]Thanks to Dr. Charles Pollard for this imagery, which is found in "This Is Not Disneyland. We Are Not on a Track," *Calvin Spark* 48, no. 3 (Fall 2002): 52-53.
[2]Bruce, *New Testament Documents*, p. 3.

11 / Community of Faithfulness

LOOKING AHEAD

MEMORY VERSE: 1 Corinthians 15:58
BIBLE STUDY: 1 Peter 1:3-25
READING: The Journey of Faith That Outlasts a Lifetime

The challenge of the church to be obediently faithful in work, witness and worship until the Lord comes again is emphasized strongly in a variety of ways in the New Testament. Because the promise of God in the whole of Scripture is sure, the church is "steadfast, immovable, always excelling in the work of the Lord," because we know that in the Lord "our labor is not in vain" (1 Corinthians 15:58 NRSV).

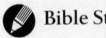 **Bible Study Guide**

After reading 1 Peter 1:3-25, spend some time reflecting on it with the following questions in mind before looking at the Reading.

1. Read 1 Peter 1:1-2, the formal introduction to this epistle. Look on a map to locate where the exiles are scattered (v. 1). How does Peter's description of his first readers include each person of the divine Trinity?

2. In 1 Peter 1:3-4 how does the word order and connections between the ideas Peter uses provide a good summary of the gospel?

3. Understanding the historical context of Peter's first readers as "exiles" who are suffering persecution for the sake of the gospel, what is the significance of how Peter describes their "inheritance" (v. 4)?

4. How does the connection between this future, heavenly inheritance (v. 4) and the faith needed by the church suffering as exiles in the first century describe the status of salvation in verse 5?

5. How does "this" (v. 6), first referred to as a "living hope" (v. 3), help those who are suffering from a variety of trials to rejoice in the midst of their circumstances (vv. 6-7)?

6. How should the promise of "praise, glory and honor when Jesus Christ is revealed" (v. 7) affect joy, faith and confidence in the gift of salvation for the believers (vv. 8-9) in their times of trial and difficult circumstances?

7. Summarize Peter's confidence in salvation in the light of God's promises given through the Old Testament prophets (vv. 10-12). Why would this be especially important to Peter in the light of his own struggle to understand who Jesus was and his own journey of faith? (Look back to Peter's story in study 1 as you consider this dynamic.)

8. There is a shift from the promises of God to the expectations of God for his people in verse 13. How does the promised revelation of Jesus Christ tie these two sections of the text together?

9. How is the behavior of "obedient children" (v. 14) described in both negative and positive ways (vv. 14-17)?

10. What does Peter highlight in verses 18-21 as the reason for living in "reverent fear" of God's judgment on "each person's work" (v. 17)?

What connection does Peter make between the security of salvation, hope, faith and glory, and how a follower of Christ is expected to live in this world?

11. What is the ultimate evidence of a believer's salvation, growth in holiness and obedience to God's Word, according to Peter in verse 22?

How does this mark of the church reflect genuine faith in God's Word, God's promises and the living hope of the inheritance outlined in this passage?

⊙ Reading: The Journey of Faith That Outlasts a Lifetime

First Peter was likely written in or near Rome in the mid-60s during a time of increased persecution during the reign of the Emperor Nero (A.D. 54–68). Silvanus, also referred to as Silas, is mentioned in 1 Peter 5:12 and is probably Peter's scribe for this letter or the bearer of the letter to its destination. Peter's first epistle is considered the finest use of Greek in the New Testament. Peter's unique authority in the church was well recognized by the early church, and this letter, and particularly the focus passage for this study, is a beautiful summary of salvation as the work of the triune God of grace and the ultimate unveiling of God's victory and the vindication of his people who have put their faith in Christ alone.

First Peter 5:13 mentions the church in "Babylon," a cryptic reference to the city of Rome.[1] Peter's idea of the church as a community of exiles fits well with his use of "Babylon," because Judaism in the Second Temple period lived within the dark historical shadow of Judah's exile to Babylon in the sixth century B.C. and the subsequent rule of Medes, Persians and Greeks, especially the violent oppression of the Greek Seleucids in Palestine. After the revolt led by the Maccabees in the second century, which gained 103 years of relative freedom (166–63 B.C.), Rome's conquest (63 B.C.) renewed the Jewish longing for a secure future free from threats and oppression. Jewish Christians struggled with significant resistance to their faith from both unbelieving Jews as well as the empire itself. Jewish Christians were the first audience for this letter, and, like that found in the letter to the Hebrews, this two-pronged struggle is particularly evident.[2] Thus, Peter writes to the predominantly Jewish Christian communities in the eastern half of Asia Minor, including the provinces to the north bordering the Black Sea, where the church was being severely persecuted at the time.

When Peter wrote this first epistle, the apostle Paul may already have perished (or soon would) under Nero's persecution. Peter may have expected the same fate in a fairly short time. This is certainly clear in 2 Peter, written shortly after the first epistle (2 Peter 1:12-14). The apostle is aware that there are fewer remaining eyewitnesses to Jesus' earthly life, teaching, crucifixion, resurrection and ascension (1 Peter 1:8), and he wants to help the church embrace not just the gospel but the importance for steadfast faithfulness in times of trial. This faith "in the trenches" will help the church fix its "eyes on Jesus" (Hebrews 12:2). Peter reminds the church that the sojourn on the way to the eternal kingdom may be long and difficult, but it ends with God's sure promise of glory.

With this background one can better appreciate Peter's reminder that the "inheritance" of those reborn "into a living hope . . . can never perish, spoil or fade" (1 Peter 1:3-4). The superiority of this inheritance, in contrast to the land promised to the children of Abraham, is clear. The inheritance of those "who through faith are shielded by God's power" (v. 5) is permanent and can't be conquered by Babylonians or Romans or any earthly empire; it is undefiled by pagan practices or religious compromise; and it doesn't grow old, wither or fade away (v. 4).[3] Suffering "all kinds of trials" with a steadfast and unwavering faith results "in praise, glory and honor when Jesus Christ is revealed" (vv. 6-7).[4] This final "unveiling" of Jesus Christ at his return will also unveil the fullness of salvation for God's people (v. 5). Salvation is complete in the person and finished work of Christ Jesus in his earthly life. Between now and then the Spirit of Christ moves the church to spread the good news of this victory throughout the world with "inexpressible and glorious joy" (v. 8).

Peter's emphasis is that God's salvation is complete and is "ready to be revealed" (v. 5) at the time of Christ's return. As New Testament scholar Peter H. Davids summarizes, "Every preparation for the final unveiling of this salvation is completed. The curtain is about to go up. Only the final signal is waited. Thus there is no question that God plans and has in fact accomplished salvation for his people, nor that the last times are here."[5]

With utmost confidence the church needs to sojourn by faith in God's promise, long affirmed by the Scripture, which will outlast all circumstances (1 Peter 1:10-12, 23-25).

This confidence in the finished work of Christ Jesus as prophesied in Scripture manifests itself in the holiness of a believer's life and an alert readiness to herald the gospel faithfully in the world (1 Peter 1:13-16; 2:1-3). This same confidence in the completeness of salvation through the blood of the Savior (1 Peter 1:17-21) demands that the eternal community of the redeemed must be marked by a deep love for one another (vv. 22-23). As pilgrims "shielded by God's power" (v. 5) and recipients of costly grace (vv. 9, 18-19), we journey together joyfully, steadfastly and lovingly toward our only true home, the kingdom of the triune God (v. 2). This, Peter says, is the Christian life. With "minds that are alert and fully sober" (v. 13) the church journeys as though on tiptoe, ready for whatever that day might bring—whether it be trials that prove our faith (vv. 6-7) or the suddenness of that final unveiling and the glorious vindication of such faith (vv. 5, 7, 13).

In 1 Corinthians 15:58, Paul summarizes the Christian life in a way very similar to Peter. Paul ends his magisterial defense of the bodily resurrection for both Christ Jesus and the church with this down-to-earth admonition concerning the need for steadfast faithfulness as we journey, ready for what the day might bring: "Therefore, my dear brothers and sisters, stand firm. Let nothing move you. Always give yourselves fully to the work of the Lord, because you know that your labor in the Lord is not in vain."

[1]John, the writer of the Revelation, also uses this term to designate the Roman Empire itself.

[2]Peter's use of the Greek Old Testament throughout the letter, in quotes as well as paraphrases, indicates the Jewish nature of his original audience. Only Romans, a much longer book, includes more Old Testament references.

[3]See also 1 Peter 5:4, where Peter mentions "the crown of glory that will never fade away." The word translated in both verses as "fade" is unique to this epistle.

[4]The word translated "revealed" is from the Greek word *apokalypsis*, which means "unveiling." Peter uses this word as an expression equivalent to that of the *parousia* or "second coming."

[5]Peter H. Davids, *The First Epistle of Peter*, in The New International Commentary on the New Testament (Grand Rapids: Eerdmans, 1990), p. 54.

Reading Study Guide

1. Create a list of all the things Peter mentions in this chapter that create confidence in the salvation of Christ Jesus and your eternal destiny in the kingdom of God. From this list, write a prayer of thanksgiving that expresses your gratitude for these promises of God's grace.

2. Consider various trials (v. 6) that you have had (or still have) in your life that have tested the steadfastness of your faith. In the light of these trials, how have you experienced both the weakness and the strengthening of your faith?

3. Consider verses 8-9 in the light of your own faith in Christ Jesus compared to those Peter addressed directly in the first century. How should the promise of "praise, glory and honor when Jesus Christ is revealed" (v. 7) affect your joy, faith and confidence in the gift of salvation today?

4. Throughout the Old and New Testaments, stories of glory and vindication always follow stories of trial and suffering. Which stories and characters in Scripture have helped your faith in times of difficulty?

The psalms often celebrate this sequence for use in worship. Psalms 27, 40, 98, 116, and 145 are good examples of this. Read one of these psalms and then write your own psalm that reflects your experience of God's faithfulness in times of trial.

5. Consider two or three things that you can do to foster a mind that is fully alert and fully sober (v. 13), which would help your sense of focus and preparedness for the return of the King. Ask someone to hold you accountable for this new or renewed commitment.

6. Take several days to finish reading 1 Peter. Summarize the major dynamics that stand out to you in this letter. With your congregation in mind, as well as its contemporary situation, note how this letter is still powerfully helpful. Share your ideas with a few friends and pray together for the work, witness and community life of your congregation as you journey together day by day.

⟳ Connecting to the Old Testament

There is a picture of life's journey tucked away in Exodus that illustrates both the steadfast promise of God and the patience needed for the faith of God's people to mature in holiness. Although historical, the exodus story of Israel's journey from Egypt and their experience in the wilderness also serves as an allegory of the believer's deliverance from the slavery of sin. Along the way both Moses and the people experienced times of discouragement and doubt. It was hard at times to believe the promise of rest in a land they had not seen. In addition, as time went on, they became very aware that this land was currently occupied by people who knew nothing of such a promise. Like believers secure in Christ's salvation, we still know what it's like to struggle with sin occupying our lives and faith communities—in Moses' story they were known as "Amorites, Hittites, Perizzites, Canaanites, Hivites and Jebusites" (Exodus 23:23) or the "Ites" for short.

The Lord tells Moses that his angel will go before them into this occupied land, but they are to take care not to "bow down before their gods or worship them or follow their practices" and be uncompromising in their allegiance to Yahweh, the God who was their Deliverer (Exodus 23:23-24). Then the text offers this startling caution to these sojourners, "I will not drive them out in a single year, because the land would become desolate and the wild animals too numerous for you. Little by little I will drive them out before you, until you have increased enough to take possession of the land" (Exodus 23:29-30).

The journey of a faithful life is secured by God's word of promise, but it is not simple or untried along the way. Like Israel with the Ites, we struggle against sin in the life of salvation. And sometimes we wonder why our progress in sanctification seems to be so slow. Well, Exodus tells us, like Peter does in the text for this study, the journey itself is part of God's goodness to us even when it doesn't seem great. God deals "little by little" with the sin in our life for the same two reasons the conquest of the Ites took a lot longer than a year. First, if we were to see all of our sin and our sin nature the way God does, we would find ourselves "desolate," overwhelmed by how truly awful we really are, how "all have sinned and fall short of the glory of God." (Romans 3:23).

Second, God takes his time with our journey of faith and growth in holiness, and only reveals to us the next Ite, the next sin to deal with when we face it with an increasingly mature faith in order to possess the promise on the other side of that struggle. Recognizing sin and its practices in our lives is not a mark of immature backsliding, but spiritual growth that has matured enough to deal with it.

God is faithful and neither the Israelites then nor Christians today travel alone. God goes before us and we travel together learning to be people of faith and love.

○ The Ancient Story and Our Story

From the beginning of God's redemptive work in history, our slow learning curve and God's patience have always been both the truth and grace of the journey. The truth is that the Christian journey is one traveled by "faith, not by sight" (2 Corinthians 5:7; see also Hebrews 11:1). God's Word is a "lamp for my feet, / a light on my path" (Psalm 119:105). Scripture shows us where we are and the direction of our next step, not a detailed blueprint of the journey itself. The next step we take by faith in the God who has given us a glimpse of the glorious destination makes it all worthwhile. The truth is that journeying by faith is not easy, but it's the only way that leads to life itself.

The grace in all of this is that, wonder of wonders, God loves us every step of the way and is committed to his work of patient sanctification in our lives. Like a good parent, our heavenly Father knows we have a lot to learn. But from the scribbles of a preschooler to the work of the mature artist, God rejoices with us in life's journey. "Little by little" we improve along the way, and God can be as pleased with the music or art or writing skills of a five-year-old as well as the final work of a mature pianist, artist or novelist. We are the work God loves, and he is patient to work out of us the very salvation that is his gift in us. Paul says it this way, "He who began a good work in you will carry it on to completion until the day of Christ Jesus" (Philippians 1:6). And Peter says, "the God of all grace, who called you to his eternal glory in Christ, after you have suffered a little while, will himself restore you and make you strong, firm and steadfast. To him be the power forever and ever" (1 Peter 5:10-11).

In his first epistle Peter is telling the church about the journey in the light of the destination. We're not there yet, but we will be. Like impatient children we tend to keep asking, "Are we there yet?" But Peter reminds us to journey well and faithfully on the road trip of life and be confident that we will arrive safely at just the right time. Then and only then will the deep magic of God's kingdom be revealed and we will finally understand that the trip was better than we ever knew.

Looking Ahead

Anticipation is often strengthened by a sense of delay. Birthday celebrations, Christmas mornings and worship on the Lord's Day are all things to look forward to because they are, in fact, not an everyday occurrence. The "living hope" (1 Peter 1:3) of a Christian is anchored in an eternal future that is more sure than any present moment of our lives. Scripture gives us a glimpse of our journey's destination, and this is the focus of our final study.

Going Deeper

The "Ites" of sin in our lives and in the world itself are often worse than we realize, and certainly worse than our individual experiences. A classic book by Cornelius Plantinga, *Not the Way It's Supposed to Be: A Breviary of Sin* (Eerdmans, 1995), is worth reading to gain not just a better understanding of sin itself but a better appreciation for the scope of God's grace in the work of salvation.

12 / Community of Joy

LOOKING AHEAD

MEMORY VERSE: 2 Peter 3:13
BIBLE STUDY: Romans 8:18-39; Revelation 21:1-5; 22:1-5
READING: Going Back Home Where We Belong

The consummation of the kingdom when Christ returns in glory to "judge the living and the dead" (Acts 10:42; 2 Timothy 4:1; 1 Peter 4:5) is manifest in the glorification of the church as the bride of Christ. The kingdom of God as an eternal reality is particular, personal and is a manifestation of the glory of Christ in the children of God. Finally at home, God's joy and our own is complete and at rest without rival or compromise, threat or brokenness.

 ## Bible Study Guide

After reading Romans 8:18-39 and Revelation 21:1-5; 22:1-5, spend some time reflecting on each with the following questions in mind before looking at the Reading.

ROMANS

1. Make note of various connections between Romans 8:18-30 and Paul's writing earlier in Romans 5:1-11 (see study 3) and Peter's address to the church in 1 Peter 1:3-25 (see study 11). What are the overarching themes these texts share in common?

2. What are the key points Paul makes concerning creation itself in Romans 8:19-22?

3. Note the repetition of the idea of "groaning" in verses 22, 23 and 26 regarding creation, believers and the Holy Spirit. What is held in common and what is distinct about each?

4. Eager expectation (v. 19), waiting eagerly (v. 23) and waiting patiently (v. 25) have the same Greek root word that reflects the idea of stretching our head or craning our neck to peek around a corner to see what comes next. What is the object of this eager longing, yearning, waiting and watching in each of these three verses?

5. In verses 26-27, how does Paul summarize the way the Spirit works to help God's children during this period of eager waiting?

6. Although God's children can't see around the corner of time, what does Paul say we surely "know" now in verses 28-39?

REVELATION

7. The first three verses of Revelation 21 begin with "I saw," "I saw" and "I heard." What did John see and hear in each experience?

8. How does Revelation 21:1-4 describe what will be changed when God (the one seated on the throne [v. 5]) makes "everything new"?

9. In Revelation 22, what does "the angel" show John in verses 1-2?

Apart from some usage in Proverbs to indicate in the broad sense a source of blessing from the righteous life, the "tree of life" (v. 2) has not been mentioned in Scripture since Genesis 2:9; 3:17-24. In light of this text in Genesis, what is being restored in this new Eden (Revelation 22)?

What is poignantly missing from this scene (v. 3)?

10. The children of God, his "servants" (v. 3), are in this place where God dwells. How does the text describe the extraordinary nearness of the people to "the throne of God and of the Lamb" in verses 3-5?

11. How does verse 5 summarize the eternal destiny of God's redeemed people?

Reading: Going Back Home Where We Belong

In study 11 it was clear that Peter's emphasis on the final revelation (unveiling) of the Lord Jesus Christ at the parousia (second coming) was intended to encourage the steadfast faith of the church in difficult times. The fullness of salvation would be revealed (1 Peter 1:5), Jesus would be revealed in glory (1 Peter 1:7, 13), and all of this is the climax of his first "unveiling" in the incarnation (1 Peter 1:20). In Romans 8 Paul focuses on what that day will do for the believer. Paul writes that "the children of God [will] be revealed" (Romans 8:19) and in this transformation finally and forever become who they really are in Christ Jesus. With the redemption of the body (Romans 8:23) our adoption into God's family is complete and we become truly and fully human, the people God always intended us to be. In this unveiling of ourselves, the children of God are "conformed to the image of his Son" (Romans 8:29) and become those who bear God's image and likeness (Genesis 1:26) without tarnish or corruption. In this final act of sanctification God's children will be unshackled from suffering in a fallen world. The God who loved us first (1 John 4:19) claimed those who belong to him before time, called them within time, has justified them through the Son of righteousness and finally will glorify forever beyond time those called according to his purpose (Romans 8:28-30; Ephesians 1:4-6). No wonder Paul says "we wait

eagerly" and yet "patiently" for such a climax (Romans 8:23, 25).

Paul's conclusion in Romans 8 is a sequence of rhetorical questions he answers himself (Romans 8:31-37) concerning how this glorious and eternal destiny should help God's children live in the light of who they are in Christ during this time of "present sufferings" (v. 18). Paul, in fact, begins this passage with such eager expectation of what will be that he says our suffering is "not worth comparing with the glory that will be revealed in us" (v. 18)! And creation just can't wait for "the children of God to be revealed" for who they really are in Christ. Creation itself "waits with eager expectation" (v. 19) for our unveiling! In the fullness of human redemption and glorification through Christ Jesus, creation will be "liberated from its bondage to decay" (v. 21) and will once again flourish in the way God always intended. Creation "has been groaning" (v. 22) since Genesis 3 and also longs to be set right. And because of the presence of the Holy Spirit, who knows the depth of what's gone wrong and the wondrous glory when all is made new, God's children join creation's groaning for the day God's adoption of his children is finalized in the redemption of our bodies (v. 23). Even beyond this, Paul says, the Spirit of God joins in "wordless groans" to help us until that day as an act of intercession on our behalf so that we can grow to understand the will of God better and to deeply trust that even in present suffering God is at work for our good (vv. 26-28).[1]

In some ways Romans 8 summarizes the good news of the whole biblical narrative. Indeed, the reality of John 3:16 is reflected in Romans 8! "God so loved the world [kosmos in Greek] that he gave his one and only Son, that whoever believes in him shall not perish but have eternal life." The creation that God declared "good" and "very good" in Genesis 1 is included in the redemptive work of the Lord Jesus Christ. The eternal destiny of God's people is an embodied reality in a "new heaven and new earth." Peter reminds the church in his second letter, "In keeping with his promise we are looking forward to a new heaven and a new earth, where righteousness dwells" (2 Peter 3:13). Just before this verse in 2 Peter, the apostle describes the cosmic transition of "the old order of things [that] has passed away" mentioned in Revelation 21:4. Peter concludes his teaching about the new heaven and new earth in 2 Peter with the practical admonition to live like people bound for such a glorious destiny just as he did in his first letter (2 Peter 3:14). In Romans Paul will do the same, but not until chapter 12. In Romans 8:31-39, Paul takes time to celebrate the wonder of our ultimate transformation into the image of God's Son and, in this sight-giving glimpse of glory, joins the victory parade of the Savior who has in his resurrection and ascension "made us more than conquerors"!

In the light of the Spirit's help and the promise of adoption in bodily redemption and the hope of glory promised by God, who gave us his Son and will see us through present suffering, Paul ends Romans 8 with a bold declaration of conviction that salvation in Christ is absolutely secure and that nothing can undo the love God has for his children bound up in the life of Christ Jesus (vv. 37-39). In the security of this glorious salvation and present promise, we are ready for a glimpse of the eternal reality of the place where "righteousness dwells" (2 Peter 3:13), God's new heaven and new earth. The ending of the revelation of Jesus Christ to John gives us that glimpse.

As the "first earth had passed away" (Revelation 21:1), the "old order of things has passed away" (Revelation 21:4). John sees the new Jerusalem, "the Holy City" of God's peace, God's shalom (v. 2) descending, coming like a bride down the aisle, to meet her groom. A loud voice declares that God's promise of old (Leviticus 26:11-12; Jeremiah 31:33) is finally a reality—God will dwell among his people (Revelation 21:3). Revelation 22:4 goes on to say that "they will see his face" in this new city! The glory of God's face that even Moses could not see during his earthly journey (Exodus 33:20, 23) is unveiled. God's "dwelling place," his tabernacle, once shrouded by curtains and hidden in the incarnation (John 1:14) is now fully open to his people unveiled, unhidden (Revelation 21:3). God is close enough to wipe away our tears, our suffering (v. 4).

In this new heaven and new earth, in this new city, new garden, there is no unsettling "sea" or turmoil (Revelation 21:1) and no darkness of fear or evil (Revelation 22:5). But there is a tree, the "tree of life" (Revelation 22:2), which had been kept from humankind, guarded by "a flaming sword flashing back and forth" lest we live forever in our sinful state (Genesis 3:22-24). In this new garden in the midst of "the city" (Revelation 22:3) this tree flourishes and yields its fruit without fail, and every tribe and nation find healing (v. 2). Ezekiel may have had a glimpse of this eternal place (Ezekiel 47:12). But in that day of days, this place will be the home of the redeemed forever. And we will drink deeply of the "water of life" (Revelation 22:1) and never thirst again. For this God's children, in union with Christ Jesus the Son by the Spirit, wait eagerly and patiently by faith and in hope.

---

[1]The Spirit, the one who knows the mind of God (Romans 8:27), knows the will of God as we pray. In Isaiah 55:8 God declares this need for God's help because God's "thoughts are not your thoughts, / neither are your ways my ways."

Reading Study Guide

1. In the light of Romans 8:18-39 and Revelation 21:1-5; 22:1-5, read all of Romans 8. Then, consider both the present reality of being "set free" in Christ and immune from all condemnation (Romans 8:1-2). How does this make a difference in how you live this day?

   How does your eternally secure destiny affect your daily life?

2. In the knowledge of God's love for the cosmos and the promised new heaven and new earth, what are several ways that Christians can honor God through caring for creation today?

3. What do you think it means for the church, the servants of God, to reign with Christ the King forever (Revelation 22:5)?

4. Write a short paragraph describing what you think heaven will be like as an eternal experience. Bear in mind that, for the most part, Scripture confines its descriptions of the eternal kingdom to the use of similes (using the word *like* or *as*) to approximate the indescribable. And remember that Paul writes that God "is able to do immeasurably more than all we ask or imagine" (Ephesians 3:20). How do the texts considered in this study help you create an answer for those who express the idea that "heaven sounds boring"?

5. How do the security of salvation and the glory of God's eternal dwelling with his people help encourage your commitment to sharing the victory of God in Christ as good news in the world today?

How does understanding the finished work of God in Christ help make your opportunity for mission (gospel demonstration) and evangelism (gospel proclamation) more joyful and less burdensome?

↻ Connecting to the Old Testament

Throughout this study it is easy to see how God's story revealed in Scripture ends in a similar place to where it begins, with a garden as a gift of God. In Scripture the garden (also *paradise*, a word derived from the Persian language) is depicted as a well-watered and cultivated area in nature and is used as a blueprint for sacred space, which is also reflected in the design and decoration of the tabernacle. The garden when "the old order of things has passed away" and all is new (Revelation 21:4-5) is a restoration of Eden, and yet something more as well. The Jewishness of the first garden that is replicated in the tabernacle is restored as the garden of God, which has the water of life as its nourishment and the tree of life that nourishes the nations, the peoples of all cultures who have found their union in Christ Jesus. The eternal garden is but a part of the eternal city, and in this eternal sacred space there is no serpent (Genesis 3), no sea, no threat, no curse (Revelation 21:1; 22:3).

In the new heaven and new earth, creation will celebrate its release from its "bondage to decay" (Romans 8:21). Isaiah prophesied the fullness of God's redemptive word when he declared that God's people

will go out in joy
    and be led forth in peace;
the mountains and hills

will burst into song before you,
and all the trees of the field
    will clap their hands.
Instead of the thornbush will grow the juniper,
    and instead of briers the myrtle will grow.
This will be for the LORD's renown,
    for an everlasting sign,
    that will endure forever. (Isaiah 55:12-13)

◯ The Ancient Story and Our Story

The culmination of God's work of grace is a salvation in which nothing "will be able to separate us from the love of God that is in Christ Jesus our Lord" (Romans 8:39). John's first epistle summarizes our relationship with God through Christ by the Spirit like this:

> This is love: not that we loved God, but that he loved us and sent his Son as an atoning sacrifice for our sins. Dear friends, since God so loved us, we also ought to love one another. No one has ever seen God; but if we love one another, God lives in us and his love is made complete in us.
>
> This is how we know that we live in him and he in us: He has given us of his Spirit. And we have seen and testify that the Father has sent his Son to be the Savior of the world. (1 John 4:10-14)

This ancient story is our story, and wonder of wonders, we will see God. And live. In 1 Corinthians 13 Paul ends his definition of love with a touch of longing for its fullest expression. He writes, "Now we see only a reflection as in a mirror; then we shall see face to face. Now I know in part; then I shall know fully, even as I am fully known" (1 Corinthians 13:12). John's vision in the Revelation promises this deep love and deep knowing: "They will see his face, and his name will be on their foreheads. . . . The Lord God will give them light" (Revelation 22:4-5).

We who in that day of days will bear God's name, conformed to the image of the Son, will know Love. And in that day we will love with a righteousness that is finally at home in the garden of God's shalom. This is the promise of Jesus: "I go and prepare a place for you, [and] I will come back and take you to be with me that you also may be where I am" (John 14:3). It is also his prayer on our behalf: "Father, I want those you have given me to be with me where I am and to see my glory, the glory you have given me because you loved me before the creation of the world" (John 17:24). Brothers and sisters, this is our living hope in Christ Jesus.

With all the questions we might have about eternal existence and our own experience of death and resurrection, it is enough for us to know Jesus lives at our Father's right hand. And we have been given his Spirit as the guarantee of a glorious inheritance. Christina Rossetti (1830–1894) puts our longing, our groaning, our questions and our hope in biblical perspective in her poem "That Where I Am, There Ye May Be Also."

> How know I that it looms lovely that land I have never seen,
> With morning-glories and heartsease and unexampled green,
> With neither heat nor cold in the balm-redolent air?
> Some of this, not all, I know; but this is so;
> Christ is there.
>
> How know I that blessedness befalls who dwell in Paradise,
> The outwearied hearts refreshing, rekindling the worn-out eyes,
> All souls singing, seeing, rejoicing everywhere?
> Nay, much more that this I know; for this is so;
> Christ is there.
>
> O Lord Christ, Whom having not seen I love and desire to love,
> O Lord Christ, Who lookest on me uncomely yet still Thy dove,
> Take me to Thee in Paradise, Thine own made fair;
> For whatever else I know, this thing is so;
> Thou art there.

Going Deeper

There is no better way to go deeper in the Word of God than to read it slowly, carefully, humbly and daily. The truth of Scripture is carried into our lives in the shape of a story that reveals the truth about God, about humankind, about redemption and eternal destiny. The Bible is a theo-drama, a play script that invites us to participate, to step on the stage of life and play the part "God prepared in advance for us to do" (Ephesians 2:10). To study the script is wise. Jesus still says to us, "Let anyone with ears to hear listen!" (Mark 4:9; 4:23; 8:18; Luke 8:8; 14:35). To know the Playwright, to trust the Director—in this is wisdom.

ALSO AVAILABLE

Discipleship Essentials
Greg Ogden
978-0-8308-1087-1, paperback, 237 pages

Leadership Essentials
Greg Ogden and Daniel Meyer
978-0-8308-1097-0, paperback, 176 pages

Witness Essentials
Daniel Meyer
978-0-8308-1089-5, paperback, 208 pages

The Essential Commandment
Greg Ogden
978-0-8308-1088-8, paperback, 204 pages

Old Testament Essentials
Tremper Longman III
978-0-8308-1051-2, paperback, 215 pages